ENCOUNTERS

THE CHRONICLES OF LUCIFER JONES

Volume I—1922-1926: Adventures

Volume II—1926-1931: Exploits

Volume III—1931-1934: Encounters

Volume IV—1934-1938: Hazards
(published by Subterranean Press)

Volume V—1938-1942: Voyages
(forthcoming from Subterranean Press)

THE CHRONICLES OF LUCIFER JONES

VOLUME III 1931-1934
ENCOUNTERS

MIKE RESNICK

an imprint of
ARC MANOR
Rockville, Maryland

The Chronicles of Lucifer Jones: Volume III—1931-1934: Encounters Copyright © 1994 by **Mike Resnick**. All rights reserved. This book may not be copied or reproduced, in whole or in part, by any means, electronic, mechanical or otherwise without written permission from the publisher except by a reviewer who may quote brief passages in a review.

This is a work of fiction. Any resemblance to any actual persons, events or localities is purely coincidental and beyond the intent of the author and publisher.

Tarikian, TARK Classic Fiction, Arc Manor, Arc Manor Classic Reprints, Phoenix Pick, Phoenix Rider, Manor Thrift, The Stellar Guild Series, The Phoenix Science Fiction Classics Series and logos associated with those imprints are trademarks or registered trademarks of Arc Manor Publishers, Rockville, Maryland. All other trademarks and trademarked names are properties of their respective owners.

This book is presented as is, without any warranties (implied or otherwise) as to the accuracy of the production, text or translation.

ISBN: 978-1-61242-036-3

www.PhoenixPick.com

**Great Science Fiction & Fantasy
Free Ebook Every Month**

**Visit the Author's Website
http://MikeResnick.com**

Published by Phoenix Pick
an imprint of Arc Manor
P. O. Box 10339
Rockville, MD 20849-0339
www.ArcManor.com

To Carol, as always,

And to Laura Resnick:
my daughter, the writer

♈

CONTENTS

CAST OF CHARACTERS	9
1. THE HOME-MADE MAN	11
2. DOUBLED AND REDOUBLED	25
3. TREASURE HUNTING	41
4. THE LOST CONTINENT	54
5. EXERCISING GHOSTS	68
6. THE WEREWOLF	79
7. THE CLUBFOOT OF NOTRE DAME	90
8. THE CROWN JEWELS	104
9. THE LOCH NESS MONSTER	121
10. A TABERNACLE IS NOT A HOME	132
11. DEATH IN THE AFTERNOON	142

CAST OF CHARACTERS

Baron Steinmetz, who creates a home-made man out of spare parts in his basement.

King Philbert of Sylvania, who bears a remarkable resemblance to our narrator.

Gustave the Book, half man, half thing, and all gambler.

Erich Von Horst, a con man's con man.

Princess Griselda, who knows what, if not who, she likes.

Mr. Tall and *Mr. Short*, who share a taste for lost continents, money, and indiscriminate bloodshed.

Sam Hightower, who forsakes the snowman biz for the ghost game.

The Count Basil de Chenza Lupo, an aristocratic werewolf.

Quesadilla, the notorious Clubfoot of Notre Dame.

Sherringford House, the world's greatest consulting detective, who is always brilliant if not always correct.

Rupert Cornwall, a very special landlord of a very special property.

El Diablo, a bull with an attitude.

And our narrator, *The Right Reverend Honorable Doctor Lucifer Jones*, a handsome, noble and resourceful Christian gentleman who has certain unresolved differences with ten separate European governments over the finer points of the law.

1. THE HOME-MADE MAN

Europe is a lot different from Africa and Asia.
For one thing, it's got a lot more Europeans living there. For another, it's got better roads and it's a little more built up. For a third, having been told by a batch of governments that totally misunderstood my motives that my presence was no longer desired on those first two land masses, I was in some danger of running out of continents while still in the prime of my young manhood.

Therefore, I made up my mind that this time I was going to keep out of trouble and obey all the nuances of the law while seeking to establish my tabernacle and pursue my vocation (which was preaching, no matter what Interpol and some of them other biased institutions said). So when the train that took me out of Asia and all the way through Russia finally came to a stop in Bucharest, I was determined that *this* time I wasn't going to spend my first night on a new continent in the local jail.

Of course, I hadn't really counted on the fact that my Silent Partner was out to test me the way He'd tested Job in times past, and that I'd lose my bankroll in the first twenty minutes of a friendly little game of chance with a pack of Gypsies just outside the railroad station. I was sorely tempted to even the odds by insinuating my own dice into the contest, but they were a swarthy looking lot who spoke in tongues and carried an awful lot of knives and didn't look like they'd appreciate an effort to bring the laws of statistical probabilities under my more direct control, and so I took my losses like a man and wandered off, looking for some place to hole up for the night.

Well, you'd be surprised how many Romanian hotels wouldn't take an I.O.U. from a man of the cloth, and eventually I wandered out toward the edge of the city, and just after it got dark I found a quiet little park, and figured I'd catch a quick forty or fifty winks there before hitting all the major banking and brokerage houses with a request for donations to my tabernacle.

Well, I was just lying there, snoring kind of gentle-like and minding my own business, when all of a sudden I opened my eyes and looked up and realized that either the stars were moving awful fast across the sky or someone was dragging me along the ground by my feet, and I looked ahead and sure enough this little hunchbacked guy was pulling me across the grass toward a wooden wagon that was attached to an old swaybacked horse.

"Hey!" I said. "What in tarnation is going on here?"

He dropped my feet like they were on fire and turned to look at me.

"You're alive!" he said.

"Of course I'm alive!" I said. "Why kind of country are you running here, anyway? Can't a man take a little nap in a public park without getting hauled off to jail?"

"This isn't a park," he said. "It's a cemetery."

"I'm the Right Reverend Honorable Doctor Lucifer Jones, and if I've busted any laws by camping out here, I'm sure we can work something out."

"It makes no difference to me," he answered. "I am Ivor. I serve the Baron Steinmetz."

"Then if you ain't some kind of night watchman, why were you dragging me off to that there wagon?" I demanded.

"I thought you were dead," said Ivor.

"The Baron pays you to go around tidying up the cemetery, does he?" I asked.

"Not exactly," said Ivor. "He sent me here to bring him back a better brain."

"He ain't pleased with the one he's got?"

Ivor sighed. "It's all very complicated, Doctor Jones."

"Yeah, it sounds a mite complicated," I allowed. "I mean, a lot of folks wish they were a little smarter, but this Baron of yours is the first one I ever heard tell of who's actually trying to do something about it."

"You don't understand, Doctor Jones," said Ivor. "He doesn't want the brain for himself."

"He's stealing it for a friend?"

Ivor shook his head. "It's for his work. He has long sought to create a living man. For years he has labored to reanimate dead tissue, putting together spare body parts in the laboratory he has built in the basement of his castle."

"Seems to me that the standard way of creating new men is cheaper and easier, not to say more fun," I said.

"He is a brilliant man," said Ivor. "A great scientist. He is on the verge of a major breakthrough."

It sounded to me like anyone who wanted to build a man in his basement was more on the verge of a major break*down*, but I just smiled and nodded sagely.

"After more than a decade of trial and error, of experiment after experiment, he had reached the final stage of his work," continued Ivor. "All he needs now is the proper brain."

"And he wanted mine?" I said. "Well, I'm flattered, Brother Ivor, but if it's all the same to you, I ain't done using it myself yet."

"I didn't know you were alive, Doctor Jones," said Ivor apologetically. "I heard that a major bookseller had died yesterday, and I thought: what a wonderful present that would make for my master—a brain that had spent its entire life immersed in literature. It's his birthday, and the brain would be such a nice surprise for him."

"Well, it seems to me that if you just stick around long enough, Brother Ivor, they'll bring this here bookman to the cemetery and plant him, and then all you got to do is mark the spot and dig him up at your leisure."

"It's not that easy," he said. "They have already arrested me twice for grave robbing. I can only sneak in here at nights, and by then the day's corpses have already been buried."

At which point my Silent Partner, who had returned from sabbatical, smote me right betwixt the eyes with another of His great big heavenly revelations.

"That ain't no problem at all, Brother Ivor," I said.

"It isn't?" he asked.

"For a small retainer, I'd be happy to hang around here til they brung this guy in, and mark the spot where they bury him."

"Oh, the Baron will be so happy!" said Ivor, clapping his little hands together.

"And for a further consideration, I'll give you a hand digging him up and delivering him to your boss."

"You have no moral compunctions about digging in hallowed ground?" he asked.

"Who better to dig in it than a man of the cloth?" I said.

"It's a deal, Doctor Jones!" he said excitedly. "I will return every night at midnight until they have brought him here and buried him."

"Sounds good to me, Brother Ivor," I said as he took his leave of me, and a couple of minutes later I was sound asleep again.

When I woke up in the morning I took a little stroll around the cemetery and found an apple orchard at the far end of it, which took care of my meals for the rest of the day. I spent the bulk of the morning and afternoon attending maybe half a dozen graveside services, and I was so moved by the sad story of a lovely young milkmaid who died of bloat after drinking her employer's entire wine cellar that I even stepped up and said a few words on her behalf myself.

Then, at about twilight, they lugged in another casket, and I moseyed over to find out the identity of the deceased.

"I don't think anyone knew his real name," said one of the gravediggers. "His headstone says he's Gustave Book."

"Where are all the mourners?" I asked.

"He didn't seem to have any friends or family, so we're burying him right now," was the answer.

"That's kind of tragic, a man devoted to books like poor old Gustave," I said.

"Well, it's not a profession designed to make you a lot of lasting friends," said the gravedigger. "A lot of people went broke at old Gustave's place of business."

I never knew anyone to go broke buying books before, but I figured Gustave must have been a dealer in rare antiquarian stuff and maybe some illuminated manuscripts and the like, and I figured he must have had a very unhappy missus, because with all the money he left her she could at least have bought him a bigger headstone and put his right name on it, but that wasn't none of my business. I just thanked the gravediggers for their information, sat down on a bench and watched 'em plant old Gustave, and then took a little constitutional around the cemetery while waiting for Ivor to show up.

He was there right at midnight, just like he'd promised, with his old swaybacked horse and his wooden cart.

"Did they bury him today, Doctor Jones?" he asked eagerly.

"You're in luck, Brother Ivor," I said. "He's been resting peaceably for the better part of six hours now."

"Excellent!" said Ivor. "Where is he?"

I led him over to the grave. "He showed up kind of late, and they barely had time to bury him before dark," I explained. "Evidently they aim to plant the headstone tomorrow."

"Let's get busy," said Ivor, tossing me a shovel.

"What's *this* for?" I asked.

"You're going to help me dig, aren't you?"

"Well, actually, I had in mind something more in the line of offering you encouragement and giving the Baron the benefit of my sage advice and worldly experience," I said.

"Ten extra American dollars," said Ivor.

"Fifty," I said.

"Fifteen," he countered.

"Tell you what," I said. "We'll split the difference. Make it an even forty and it's a deal."

Well, we haggled for another five minutes, and I finally agreed to apprentice at the grave-robbing trade for $34.29. It took us the better part of two hours to dig down to old Gustave, and then we found that we weren't strong enough to pull his casket out of the hole, so we unlatched it and I kind of climbed in with him and handed him up to Ivor, who dragged him by the feet over to the cart and loaded him up. Then we spent another hour putting all the dirt back and patting it down nice and neat, and finally we climbed into the cart and the old horse started trotting along the empty streets.

"He sure looks calm and peaceful, lying there staring up at the moon like he is," I said, turning in my seat to get my first real good look at Gustave.

"I wonder what he died of," said Ivor. "I hope it wasn't anything catching."

I opened Gustave's formal jacket and took a quick peek. "Looks like he was shot to death," I said.

"It sounds painful," said Ivor with a shudder.

"I don't believe he felt the last twenty or thirty bullets at all," I said, buttoning his coat back up.

"Why would anyone want to kill a bookseller?" mused Ivor.

"Beats the hell out of me, Brother Ivor," I admitted. "I know you Europeans are degenerate and sadly lacking in Christian virtues, but that seems an awfully stern punishment for overcharging."

Well, he didn't say nothing to that, and we rode in silence for about half an hour, til we left the city limits and got out into the suburbs, and pretty soon we came to a rocky hill, and there on top of it was this huge castle.

"The Baron will be so happy to meet you!" said Ivor. "I told him how you had agreed to help us."

"I'm always happy to help advance the cause of science," I said modestly.

"Tonight we will witness the culmination of his life's work," continued Ivor. He leaned over and added confidentially. "He is delighted that you are a man of the cloth. He wants you to baptize his creation."

"Well, a critter what's made of twenty or thirty other men ain't the easiest thing in the world to baptize," I said. "I figure we'll have to baptize each part separately, at maybe five dollars a shot, just to be on the safe side. Can't have his left elbow doing evil things when the rest of him is trying to serve the Lord, if you see what I mean."

"Money is no object to the Baron," answered Ivor.

"You don't say?" I replied. "I don't suppose he wants his castle blessed too, just to cover all the bases?"

"You'll have to speak to him about it," said Ivor, as the horse starting climbing a little path in the hill. "We're almost there."

We reached a huge wrought iron gate and Ivor got out and rang a bell, and a moment later the gate opened inward just long enough to let us through, and then slammed shut behind us. Ivor guided the horse up to the huge front door, and then we stopped and climbed down off the wagon, and the door opened, and out stepped this real skinny guy with wide staring eyes. He was wearing some kind of a laboratory coat, and he was smoking a Turkish cigarette that was stuck in a long gold holder.

He walked over to the back of the wagon and looked at Gustave.

"Excellent, excellent," he murmured. "You have done well this night, Ivor." Then he turned to me. "You are Doctor Jones?"

"The Right Reverend Doctor Lucifer Jones, at your service," I said.

"I am Baron Steinmetz," he said. "Ivor has told me how you have aided my cause. I wish to thank you."

"Well, I had in mind something just a tad more substantial than a handshake," I said.

"I quite understand, and you will not find me ungrateful, Doctor Jones. But first let us bring the body inside and prepare for the final transformation."

The three of us lifted old Gustave out of the wagon and carried him into the castle, which was huge and cold and kind of damp and made of stone and lit by candles.

"This way," said the Baron, heading off for a staircase that led down to the basement. We almost lost Gustave a couple of times as the stairs kept curving around corners, but finally we made it to the next level, and found ourselves in a big laboratory, filled with all kinds of gizmos that didn't make no sense to me but were humming and glowing to beat the band.

We laid Gustave on a wood table and then the Baron took me by the arm and led me over to another table, which was covered with a big blanket. He reached down and pulled the blanket off, revealing a huge body lying there. Parts of it didn't seem to quite fit, and there were stitches and electrodes everywhere, and the top of its skull was missing.

"Well, Doctor Jones," said the Baron. "What do you think?"

"You wouldn't happen to have something in a blonde of the female persuasion, would you?" I said. "Maybe a size eight?"

"All in good time," he said. "One day I shall turn out beauty queens galore, but first we must complete the prototype. He lacks only a brain to be a completely functioning human being."

"That ain't never stopped certain select politicians and constabularies I've known," I offered.

"This one will be a worthy representative, I assure you," said the Baron. He turned to Ivor. "*If* you got the right brain this time."

"*This* time?" I asked.

"I don't know how it keeps happening, but the first four brains he obtained were abnormal."

"Just poor luck," said Ivor.

"It not only held back my moment of triumph, but it played hell with my fire insurance premiums."

"How can an abnormal brain affect your fire insurance?" I asked.

"The locals keep trying to burn the castle down," answered the Baron. "They simply cannot comprehend the importance of my work." He paused. "Of course, I can see their side of it, too. Number

Three *did* kill seventeen of them and tear down the local church, right after Number Two destroyed the school."

"Don't forget Number One," said Ivor.

"He simply lacked empirical knowledge," said the Baron. "I mean, how was *he* to know that all those people couldn't survive after he threw them off the belltower? He himself was incapable of feeling pain."

"I almost hate to ask," I said, "but what happened to Number Four?"

"I don't care to discuss it," said the Baron, and walked over to begin work removing Gustave's brain.

"He's kind of sensitive about Number Four," whispered Ivor.

"How come?" I asked.

"It ran off with his wife," said Ivor. "Last postcard we got from them, they were living it up on the Riviera." He paused. "But this time will be different. This time we've got the brain of a man who spent his whole life with books, who even took literature itself as part of his name."

"Done!" announced the Baron after another couple of minutes. "Now we simply transfer the brain to my creation, attach all the ganglia and synapses, and it is accomplished."

"What do you plan to call this critter?" I asked, as he placed the brain in a metal pan and carried it over.

"I really hadn't considered that," said the Baron. "I just assumed we'd call him The Monster, just like the other four."

"Ain't that likely to upset his delicate bookish feelings?" I said.

"You're quite right, Doctor Jones," said the Baron. "Ivor, what shall we call him?"

"Creature Number Five?" suggested Ivor.

"Why not just call him Gustave?" I said. "After all, that's the name he's responded to all his life."

"Gustave?" repeated the Baron distastefully. "What a dreadful name!"

"What's wrong with it?" I asked.

"I've only known one Gustave in my life, and if I never see him again, it will be too soon."

"Why not wait til you bring him back to life and ask him what he wants to be called?" said Ivor.

"A capital suggestion!" said the Baron. He turned to me. "I'll be at least half an hour transplanting and connecting the brain, Doctor Jones."

"That long, huh?"

"Well, it *is* delicate surgery," he said. "Why don't you freshen up and have Ivor get you some food in the meantime?"

"Sounds good to me," I said. "Ivor, where's the kitchen?"

"Right above us," said Ivor. "I hope you like apples."

"Why?"

"The Baron is a vegetarian. That's all we have in the house."

"Maybe I'll just settle for a quick shave and shower," I said.

"Well, that poses another problem," said Ivor apologetically. "This is an *old* castle. We don't have any running water."

"Perhaps none of that will be necessary," said the Baron, working away at the top of the monster's head. "If I just take *this* shortcut, and bypass these two synapses...Yes! It's done!"

"You got him all hooked up that fast?" I said.

"Well, he'll be tone deaf, and I rather suspect he won't be able to play rugby, but except for that, he should function just perfectly."

"I hope so," said Ivor. "Remember Number Three? He kept smelling colors and stuffing candy bars into his ear."

"We learn from our mistakes," said the Baron, starting to connect a bunch of wires to all these metal bits and pieces that were sticking out of the monster. "That is how we avoid making them again and again."

Well, I couldn't see that a batch of brand-new mistakes in a ten-foot-tall monster was all that preferable to the same old ones, but it wasn't none of my business, so I just kept quiet and watched while the Baron finished wiring his creation.

"All is in readiness," he said after another minute or two, and walked to a big metal switch on the wall. "Ivor, Doctor Jones—stand back please."

He didn't have to ask me twice, and I backed up against the wall, which had a damp and chilly feel to it, and then he pulled the switch and every gizmo in the place started buzzing and whistling, and just about the time I was sure he was gonna blow every fuse in the castle he pushed the switch back to its starting position.

All three of us walked over to the table, and son of a gun if the monster wasn't breathing. The Baron disconnected all the wires and pulled out a stethoscope and listened to its heart for a while, and the critter's eyelids kind of fluttered a bit and suddenly I was staring into its wide, wondering eyes, one brown and one blue.

"Where am I?" asked the monster.

"You're perfectly safe," said the Baron. "You are the late Gustave Book, and I am the Baron Theodore von Steinmetz. I have reanimated you here in the lower recesses of my castle."

"I'm not Gustave Book," said the monster. "I'm Gustave *the* Book." It paused while the Baron suddenly turned white as a sheet. "Steinmetz, Steinmetz..." it muttered, and suddenly it sat up. "Steinmetz, you owe me three hundred pounds sterling!"

"What are you talking about?" demanded Ivor.

"Nobody welches out on a bet with Gustave the Book," said the monster. "Let's have it."

Suddenly the Baron turned to Ivor and started hitting him on the top of his head.

"Idiot!" he screamed. "Fool! I ask for a dealer in literature, and you bring me the local bookmaker! I *thought* he looked familiar!"

"You," said Gustave to me. "Tell me what the hell is going on around here! Why is my voice different? Why does everyone look so small? Since when does my left hand have six fingers? What has happened to me?"

"You were dead, and the Baron brung you back to life," I said.

"Well, a form of pseudo life, anyway," corrected the Baron.

"I don't believe it."

"Maybe we could all sing you a rousing chorus or two of 'Happy Birthday,' to kind of put you in the mood," I said.

"Just a minute," said Gustave. He closed his eyes, then opened them again. "The last thing I remember was seeing a car go by, and then a tommy gun was pumping bullets into me, and then everything went blank. How come I'm not dead and buried?"

"Well, actually you were," I said. "Until we unburied you a couple of hours ago. In fact," I added, "there's probably them what would say you still are."

"Buried?"

"Dead," I said.

"I'm going to need some time to consider all this," said Gustave.

"You have all of eternity," said the Baron. "Being dead already, it is impossible for you to age."

"Don't bet on it," muttered Gustave. "I think I've aged thirty years in the past three minutes."

"I must write this up in my journal," said the Baron. "Ivor, you and Doctor Jones stay with him, and don't let him get excited."

He left the laboratory, and Gustave turned back to me.

"Do I look as terrible as I think I look?" he asked.

"Well, that all depends," I said.

"On what?"

"On what you think you look like."

"Like the ugliest living thing on the face of the earth," he said.

"Worse," I answered.

"Well, I suppose I haven't got too much to complain about," he said at last. "I could be back in that grave you dug me out of."

"That's the spirit, Brother Gustave," I said. "Look on the bright side. The ladies may not beat a path to your door, but at least you ain't still pushing up daisies."

"But what am I to do with myself?" he asked.

"Seems to me like you're in prime shape to become a professional rassler," I said.

"He could be a weightlifter or a basketball player," suggested Ivor.

"Right," I said. "You been looking at this through jaundiced eyes, Brother Gustave. There's no end of things you can do when you're ten feet tall and weigh six hundred pounds."

He shook his head. "I can't let anyone see me looking like this."

"Actually," said Ivor, "I believe that the Baron plans to put you on exhibition."

"I'm not going to play the freak just to satisfy his ego," answered Gustave. "I'll kill myself first."

"It's too late for that," said Ivor sympathetically. "You're already dead."

"Right," he said. "I keep forgetting." He paused. "On the other hand, if I'm already dead, he can't threaten or force me to do anything."

"Mighty few people of your particular physical attributes get forced to do anything they don't want to do," I agreed.

"Why did he use so many spare parts?" asked Gustave. "Doesn't he realize how much a new wardrobe will cost me?"

"I don't think that was among his primary concerns," said Ivor.

"I might have guessed as much from a man who won't pay off his gambling debts," muttered Gustave. "He walks into my establishment, loses three hundred pounds playing poker, writes an I.O.U., and then refuses to honor it."

"There was a reason for that," said a voice from behind us, and we all turned to see that the Baron had reentered the laboratory.

"Let's hear it," said Gustave. "I could use a good laugh after the day I've had."

"The game was rigged."

"I've never run a rigged game in my life!" said Gustave.

"Do you know the odds on someone beating me in a five-man game with the hand I held?" said the Baron.

"Yeah," said Gustave. "32,457 to one."

"How did you know that?" asked the Baron.

"Numbers are my business."

"Really? I'm terrible with them myself."

"I can tell," said Gustave, holding his arms out in front of him. One was a good six inches longer than the other.

"Quick," said the Baron. "How much is 358 times 409?"

"146,422," said Gustave.

"How are you at calculus?" asked the Baron.

"I've done my fair share of it in school."

"Have you studied any other higher mathematics?"

"Oh, not really," said Gustave modestly. "I helped Einstein a bit when he passed through here. And Schwarzschild wanted to call it the Gustave Radius, but I told him that he had done most of the initial work and it should really be the Schwarzschild Radius." He sighed. "I never could help Schroedinger understand those damned cats, though."

"My God, man!" said the Baron, his eyes wide. "Why have you been hiding in a bookie joint?"

"I haven't been hiding," answered Gustave. "it's just deadbeats like you who can't find me."

"But why aren't you a scientist?"

"I had to loan Albert rent money last month," said Gustave. "Does that answer your question?"

"But think of the inestimable service you could be to humanity!" said the Baron.

"That didn't interest me even when I was human," said Gustave. "So why should I care now?"

"Don't you understand?" said the Baron. "I want you to work with me! I'll make you a full partner!"

"You mean you'll give me half of a run-down castle?" said Gustave. "Don't make me laugh."

"What do you want to come to work with me?"

"First," said Gustave, "I want to start my business up again. We'll run it out of Castle Steinmetz."

"What else?"

"I want my three hundred pounds."

"Done."

"One more thing," said Gustave. "The next thing we work on is a wife for me."

"Certainly," said the Baron. "With your input, I should be able to create an exact replica of Mary Pickford."

"I'll settle for Mabel Normand," said Gustave.

"Here," said the Baron. "Go over my notes while I get your money."

He tossed a stack of papers onto the table next to Gustave and raced from the room. Gustave started going over them, making little corrections here and there and muttering to himself. The Baron returned a minute later and handed him three hundred pounds.

"Well?" said the Baron eagerly. "What do you think?"

"We have a lot of work to do," said Gustave.

"Oh?"

Gustave pointed to a line on the paper. "Either 5 times 7 equals 38, or Mary Pickford is going to have feathers."

"But if you change this notation *here*," said the Baron, pointing to another of Gustave's scribblings, "she not only won't have feathers, she'll be bald as an egg."

"It's only fitting," said Gustave, "since *this* equation will eliminate her arms and legs."

Ivor kind of signaled to me, and I walked over to him.

"I know better than to interrupt the master when he's like this," he said, "so I will pay you what we owe you." He slipped me a wad of bills. "Thank you for your help, Doctor Jones."

"Any time, Brother Ivor," I said, counting the money and then putting it away in my pocket.

"Will you be staying in Bucharest?" he asked.

"No, I don't think so," I said. "From what I can see, the Baron's got the god biz pretty well under control without no help from me, so I'd best be off to seek fame and fortune elsewhere."

I followed him to the stairs, and was just starting to climb up out of the laboratory when I heard the Baron say, "So what's *wrong* with giving her three of them?"

And then Gustave paused for a moment and said, "Not a damned thing, now that I come to think of it."

I left the two of them plotting out the shape of things to come, and that was the last I ever saw of Baron Steinmetz and his homemade man…but I guess they got along pretty well together, because I did hear a couple of years later of a Romanian burleyque dancer who had three of what most women generally settle for two of.

2. DOUBLED AND REDOUBLED

You know how some people are connoisseurs of fine art or rare books or gourmet food?
Well, I seem to have become a connoisseur of jails.
The jailhouse back in Moline, Illinois is kind of a community gathering place on Saturday nights. The Johannesburg jail is pretty friendly, but the food lacks a little something. The Cairo jail is noisy and crowded. The Nairobi jail is hot and stuffy. The jail in Beria, over in Mozambique, is kind of cramped and smells of raw sewage. The Hong Kong jail smells of dead fish. The jail at Poshan is well appointed, and the jailor's got a weak spot for games of chance, but if you can't eat with chopsticks you're out of luck.
But the strangest jail I ever spent a night in was unquestionably the jail in Sylvania, a tiny kingdom which probably ain't on any map printed in the past half century. It seems they'd built this particular hoosegow with the thought of filling it to the brim with criminals, but the people of Sylvania were a pretty law-abiding lot, and although the jail had been standing for seven years, I was its first customer. The jailor was so glad to have a little company that he moved a four-poster bed into my cell, and his wife started fixing me a six-course meal every three hours.
How I came to be in the Sylvania jail was a matter of some mystery to me, because I was still bound and determined not to break no laws or otherwise impede my progress toward constructing my tabernacle and bringing all these degenerate Europeans back to the straight and narrow path. So when I hit Sylvania, with Baron Steinmetz's money still pretty much intact, I disdained all games

of chance, and instead moseyed over to the Royal Hotel and ordered up the biggest suite in the house, intent on washing the dust from my body and grabbing a good night's sleep before I went out looking for donations or shapely female assistants or whatever else I thought the tabernacle might need.

I probably should have figured something was a little strange when the desk clerk looked at me with wide, staring eyes, gulped a couple of times, and said that of course I didn't have to pay for the room, but I make it a point never to look no gift horses in the mouth. And when a passel of waiters brung up some pheasant under glass and caviar and champagne and wheeled it into my lounge with compliments of the house, I just assumed they were being polite to a man of the cloth.

Still, since everyone was being so all-fired nice to me, I decided to test the waters, as it were, and ask one of the waiters to send up a friendly young Sylvanian lady to help me pass the long lonely hours of the night. He just took it right in stride and asked me if I preferred blondes or brunettes or redheads, and I allowed that I was equally fond of all of 'em, and about half an hour later in came one of each.

And just as the four of us were getting to know each other and I was thinking that Sylvania was about the most hospitable country that I ever did visit, in burst two guys in tuxedos and two more in military uniforms, and they chased the young ladies out and told me to get dressed and carted me off to the calaboose without so much as a by your leave.

But like I said, the jail was well appointed and the service was better than I'd paid for in a batch of hostelries, so except for lacking a little company of the female persuasion and wondering what particular laws I had broken, I wasn't exactly discommoded at my current situation, and truth to tell I was eating better than I'd eaten since I'd arrived in Europe.

Then, at about noontime, two of the guys who'd arrested me the night before came to pay me a visit. One of 'em was still in his military uniform, all glittering with medals and sporting a general's insignia, and the other was dressed in a dour gray business suit. They nodded to the jailor, who let them into the cell with me and then left the building.

"Well, Heinrich," said the General, "what do you think?"

Heinrich peered intently at me through a monocle. "It's remarkable," he said at last. "Absolutely remarkable."

"I agree," said the General. "Even here, in the light of day, no one could tell the difference."

"But it's such an audacious scheme," protested Heinrich.

"It will work," said the General adamantly.

"Excuse me for interrupting," I said, "but would you gents like to tell me what I'm doing here, a clean-cut God-fearing Christian who ain't never broke a law in his life?"

"My apologies," said the General. "But it was absolutely essential that we speak to you before anyone else laid eyes on you."

"It wasn't exactly the laying on of eyes that got so rudely interrupted last night," I pointed out.

"We forgive you for that," said Heinrich.

"Well, I'm sure that's right generous of you," I said, "but I hadn't quite got around to doing anything I need to be forgiven for, if you understand my subtle but outraged meaning."

"Forget all that," said the General. "We have important business to discuss with you."

"Yeah?" I said.

He nodded. "You could be the answer to our prayers."

"Well, you're in luck, General," I said. "Answering prayers is one of the very best things I do, me being a man of the cloth and all."

"You may be in luck, too, Reverend Jones," said the General. "We have a job for you. It's dangerous, but the pay is excellent, and you'll know that you are serving the cause of Right and Justice."

"Uh...back up a couple of steps to the dangerous part," I said.

"I won't deceive you," said the General. "Your life will be constantly at risk."

"Well, it sure has been nice chatting with you fellers," I said, getting to my feet and walking to the door of my cell. "But I think it's time for me to hit the road."

"A quarter of a million dollars," said the General.

"On the other hand," I said, walking back to my bed and sitting back down on the edge of it, "it would be rude to leave without at least hearing you out."

"I don't know," said Heinrich. "Are you *sure* this is our only option?"

"We both know it is," answered the General. He turned to me. "We've yet to be formally introduced. I am General Gruenwald, head of Sylvania's army, and this is Lord Mayor Heinrich Rembert."

"Pleased to meet you," I said. "Let's talk about the half million dollars."

"All in good time, Reverend Jones," said the General. He pulled a photograph out of his pocket and handed it over to me. "Do you recognize the man in this picture?"

"It's me," I said. "But I sure can't remember posing in all them fancy duds. It must have been took at a carnival or something when I was on a bender."

"It is *not* you," said General Gruenwald. "It is a photograph of King Philbert of Sylvania, and it was taken two weeks ago."

"You don't say!"

"We *do* say," replied Lord Mayor Rembert. "You could be his double, Reverend Jones. The same weak chin, the same unkempt hair, the same look about the eyes that inspires instant mistrust, even the same slovenly way of walking."

"All right," I said. "I look like King Philbert. So what?"

"An attempt was made to assassinate Philbert the night before last," said General Gruenwald. "He still lives, but he is in the hospital, and will be confined there for at least a month. We believe that the attempt on his life was made by Wilhelm Von Sykoff, the leader of the opposition party. Von Sykoff is an evil man, totally opposed to everything King Philbert stands for. He has begun spreading the rumor that Philbert is dead, and if the people start to believe him, it will totally destabilize the kingdom. Yet the doctors will not permit Philbert any visitors, not even the members of our press, nor would it do any good, since he is swathed in bandages from head to toe and cannot possibly be recognized even by those nearest and dearest to him." He paused. "Do you see where this is leading, Reverend Jones?"

"You want to pay me a quarter of a million dollars to say a prayer for him?" I asked.

"We want you to impersonate him," said Mayor Rembert. "To *become* King Philbert for the next four weeks. To wear his clothes, make his speeches, eat his meals, sleep in his bed."

"If you can carry off this illusion until Philbert is healthy enough to resume his duties, you will save the kingdom," added General

Gruenwald. "And for this we are prepared to pay you the sum of two hundred and fifty thousand American dollars."

"Of course," continued Lord Mayor Rembert, "we would be less than candid if we did not warn you that Wilhelm Von Sykoff will probably redouble his efforts to kill you."

"Why don't you just lock him away in some dungeon somewhere?" I asked.

"He is not without his followers," said General Gruenwald. "Any such action would instantly precipitate a civil war."

"Well, Reverend Jones," said Lord Mayor Rembert, "will you do it?"

I mulled on it for a minute, and decided that even if I couldn't lock Von Sykoff away, maybe I could make him my ambassador to Tasmania or Fiji or some place like that and be rid of him for the month I had to pretend to be Philbert.

"Well," I said at last, "I ain't never been king of my very own country, and my tabernacle could sure use that money. Put half of it up front and you got yourself a deal."

"In King Philbert's—ah, *your* bedroom there is a metal box in the top drawer of your dresser," said General Gruenwald. "The down payment will be there waiting for you by this evening."

"Perhaps you should tell him that's not *all* that will be waiting for him," suggested the Lord Mayor.

The General nodded. "I'd almost forgotten about Princess Griselda."

"Princess Griselda?" I repeated.

"She is your—um, *Philbert's* betrothed. The wedding is scheduled for next spring."

"*That* will be your most severe test as Philbert's impersonator," said the Lord Mayor. "Do you think you can handle it?"

"I'm quite a hand with the ladies," I said. "Except for the improvement, she'll never know the difference."

"Then I suppose we'd best get to work," said General Gruenwald. "We'll have to sneak you into the palace and get you dressed in Philbert's clothes. Since everyone knows Philbert was shot two days ago, it might be best to keep one arm in a sling, or perhaps affect a limp." He paused. "I'll be at your side night and day to point out who you know, what their names are, what Philbert would do in given situations."

"Well, I appreciate that, General Gruenwald," I said. "Especially during the days. But," I added, thinking of Griselda, "I got a feeling that I can handle the nights on my own."

"As you wish," said General Gruenwald. He led me to the door of my prison cell. "The sooner we begin, the sooner we'll know if this audacious impersonation will work."

"Sounds good to me," I said, falling into step beside him.

We walked out to a car that had all its back windows covered up, and then climbed into it and began driving through the winding, stone-covered streets of Sylvania, passing a number of churches and taverns along the way, until we pulled up to this huge palace with gargoyles peering down at the liveried doormen. We zipped around to the servants' entrance just next to the kitchen, and they snuck me up the stairs before anyone even knew we were there.

A minute later I was standing in this room that was only slightly smaller than Lumpini Stadium back in Siam. Almost all the furniture was painted gold along the edges and covered with velvet, and the walls were loaded with paintings by some Dutchman who I figured was a friend of the family since I'd seen dance-hall posters that had more accurate renderings of what people looked like. There was a mahogany table that could have sat the whole of the Chicago White Sox, along with their manager and coaches, for dinner. Off to one side was a private cinema theater, but since General Gruenwald hadn't never heard of Theda Bara or Clara Bow, I figured I'd give it a pass. And finally there was a bedroom, with a huge four-poster bed that Solomon and all his wives could have bounced around on at the same time. The bathroom held a tub you could go sailing in, and a shower with five nozzles for them what didn't have time for a long, leisurely wallow.

"Well?" said General Gruenwald.

I allowed that I could get used to my surroundings without putting forth an enormous effort.

"Let's get you dressed properly," said the Lord Mayor, walking to a closet in which Baron Steinmetz could have stashed a couple of hundred of his home-made men. He pulled out an outfit and tossed it over to me. "Here," he said. "Change into this."

When I was done, I looked at myself in one of the dozen or so mirrors and I must admit that I was mightily impressed. My jacket, which stopped at the waist, had gold epaulettes and braid, and maybe five pounds' worth of medals, and the shiniest brass buttons

I ever did see, and my pants were deep blue with a gold stripe down the side. My boots were soft, and polished within an inch of their lives.

"And now your sword," said the General, attaching it around my waist.

"Uh…this Philbert ain't prone to sword fighting when he has too much to drink or loses his temper, is he?" I asked.

"Certainly not," said the General. "It's merely for show. Although he *is* a master swordsman."

"And now," said the Lord Mayor, "it's time to go downstairs for dinner."

We walked out the door of my suite and down a huge winding staircase. There was a little guy in glasses waiting at the bottom.

"Am I supposed to know him?" I whispered.

"He's a reporter," answered the General.

"What do I say to him?"

"Be vague and noncommittal."

When we reached the end of the staircase, the little feller walked up to me.

"How are you feeling, King Philbert?" he asked.

"I'm fit as a bull moose," I said.

"I had heard you were badly wounded," he said.

"Well, let me amend that," I said. "I'm fit as a bull moose what's been gut shot."

"I thought you were shot in the leg."

"I was," I said quickly.

"Then why do you compare yourself with a bull moose that has been gut shot?"

"Because I ain't never made the acquaintance of a moose that's been shot in the leg," I said. He just kind of stared at me, so I figured I'd change the subject. "Lovely day, ain't it?" I asked him.

"What do you plan to do about Wilhelm Von Sykoff's tax bill?" he said.

"Think it may rain, though," I said.

"All right, King Philbert," he said with a sigh. "As long as you feel compelled to discuss the weather, what do you think of it?"

"Oh, I approve of weather," I said. "And as long as I'm the king, we're gonna have it."

He was about to ask me something else when the General led me into the dining room.

There were a bunch of people there, all decked out to the nines, and the minute I entered the room they all bowed. I didn't quite know what to do, so I bowed back, which set 'em all to bowing again. I figured maybe we could just keep doing it all night long and not have to get around to talking at all, but the General nudged me and whispered that I should sit down, so I did, and then everyone else sat down too.

"I am pleased to see Your Majesty looking so well," said a large, burly man with a black mustache and lambchop sideburns.

"Well, I could stand to lose maybe a pound and a half," I said modestly.

"I mean, you seem to have recovered from your unfortunate accident."

"It takes more than forty or fifty bullets to keep a good man down," I answered.

"Careful," whispered the General. "That's Von Sykoff."

"Have you any idea who was behind this heinous act?" asked Von Sykoff.

"Oh, probably some disgruntled retard who envies my manly good looks," I said. "It ain't worth worrying about. Now let's all dig in and grab some grub."

"Such quaint Americanisms," chuckled a lady, and I turned to see I was sitting next to one of the prettier females it had ever been my privilege to see. "You are such a wit, Philbert!"

"The Princess Griselda," whispered the General.

"Why, thanks, Griselda honey," I said.

She shot me a smile that made me right anxious for dinner to end, and then Von Sykoff spoke up again.

"Has Your Majesty given any further consideration to my tax bill?" he asked.

"Not really," I said. "How much do you owe?"

Everyone kind of laughed at that, except for Von Sykoff, who turned a bright red.

"Your Majesty is in a rare humor this evening," he said through gritted teeth.

"You think that's funny?" I said. "Have you ever heard the one about the dancing girl and the Albanian priest?"

Well, I shared that little drollery with them, and then I told 'em about the traveling salesman and the architect's daughter, and then I topped it off with the tale of the airplane pilot and the Chinese virgin, and even though I forgot the punch line everyone laughed fit to kill, and it suddenly occurred to me that I *liked* being King, and that if old Philbert wanted to spend an extra couple of months recuperating it wouldn't bother me none at all.

"This is a side of you I've never seen before," said Griselda when I was all done telling my stories. "Where did you ever learn such risqué tales?"

"Griselda, honey," I said, "you wouldn't believe how many sides of me you ain't seen yet. After we get rid of all these here guests, I'll take you upstairs and show you some of them."

She just giggled like I was telling another joke, and then the waiters brought out dessert, and eventually we were all through eating, and then the General got up and proposed a toast to me, and everyone stood up and yelled "Long live Philbert!" and we all drank up, and then the Lord Mayor did the same, and then Griselda got up and drank to my health, and I began to see that even if the people weren't a hundred percent in favor of having a king instead of a president, it could break every liquor company in Sylvania if they ever changed the political system.

"Suggest that we repair to the drawing room," whispered the General after eight or nine more toasts.

"Folks," I said, getting kind of shakily to my feet, since I'd been matching 'em all toast for toast, "I just been informed that the drawing room's broke and in need of repair. Let's all mosey over there and see if we can fix it."

Everyone chuckled again, and I could see that Philbert never had to worry about people laughing at his jokes, even when he wasn't necessarily making 'em, and then I stared at everyone and they all stared back at me, and finally the General jabbed me in the short ribs and I jumped up, and then everyone else got up and we all wandered over to the drawing room, which was filled with fancy chairs and dinky little tables but didn't have no drawing materials or even pencils that I could see.

I was about to amuse the guests with some more stories, but a bunch of guys with violins started strolling around the room. They finished when they were right in front of me, and I figured I should probably reach into my pocket and tip 'em for their trouble, but they just bowed and thanked me for letting 'em perform and walked off to the kitchen or wherever it was they'd come from.

One by one the guests started leaving, until there was no one left except Griselda and Von Sykoff, and he came over and stood in front of me and stared at me.

"You seem somehow different tonight, Your Majesty," he said kind of suspiciously.

"Yeah?" I asked. "In what way?"

"Your manner of expressing yourself, for one thing."

"It's all the rage in Moline, Illinois," I said.

"How very witty," he said with an oily smile. He bowed, and suddenly lowered his voice to a whisper. "You may fool the others, but not Wilhelm Von Sykoff. Your days are numbered, imposter."

Then he turned on his heel and left before I could tell the General what he'd said.

"He's right," said Griselda.

"You know it too?" I asked.

"That you're witty?" she said. "Absolutely. It was a very pleasant change, Philbert. You seemed so tense and stern last week."

"Probably my boots were too tight," I said.

She stood up and walked over to me. "There's a beautiful moon out tonight," she said. "Shall we go for a walk?"

"Why the hell not?" I agreed.

"Philbert, you never used vulgarisms before," said Griselda.

"Well, they came cheap and they played nice music," I said, taking her arm and heading for the front door.

"I think I'd better accompany you, Your Majesty," said the General, joining us.

"I got the situation well in hand," I said.

"It is my job to protect you."

"You protect me from Princess Griselda and you just might find out what it's like to be a private again," I said.

"But..."

"I'm the King, ain't I?" I said. "And the King says: scram."

He backed away, and we went outside, and Griselda turned to me. "You seem so different tonight, Philbert," she said. "So forceful."

"What's the point of being King if I can't voice a few terse commands as the mood strikes me?" I said.

"But you've never behaved like that to General Gruenwald before."

"Let him get his own Princess," I said, giving her a friendly little pinch in a delicate area.

She shrieked. "Philbert!"

"Just being boyishly playful, my love," I said.

"You mustn't do that again until we're married," she said severely.

Which was when I began to see that old Philbert's love life hadn't yet left the starting gate.

"Refresh my memory," I said. "Just how long have we been engaged?"

"Since you were five and I was two," she answered. "But you know that."

"I also know it's about time we brung this here courtship into the twentieth century."

"What's come over you, Philbert?" she demanded.

"Probably it was getting shot by all them bullets," I said. "It makes a man realize just how fleeting life is."

"I *knew* there was some reason for this strange behavior," she said. "Does it hurt much?"

"Only when I breathe in and out," I said.

"You poor man!" she said. "And here I am, thoughtlessly making you walk around the grounds and expend your energy only two days after that frightful experience."

"Now as I come to think on it," I said, "I probably would feel a mite better if I went up to bed."

"Certainly," she said. "Let's turn around and go right back inside."

"I don't want to disturb General Gruenwald and the Lord Mayor none," I said. "Why don't we mosey around to the back entrance?"

"If you wish," she said.

We reached the stairs in the back a couple of minutes later, and I turned to her and shook her hand.

"Thanks, Griselda," I said. "You've been right understanding about my condition."

"Can you make it up the stairs yourself?" she asked.

"I made it up to the seventh stair this afternoon before I collapsed," I said. "I feel a lot stronger now. I can probably make it to the tenth or even the eleventh before I have to crawl the rest of the way."

She put my arm around her shoulders. "I'll help you," she said.

"No," I said. "Fun's fun, but I can't have a full-blooded princess compromising her reputation on my behalf, even though there ain't no one here to see us."

"Just be quiet and save your strength," she said, helping me up the first stair.

Well, it took some work, but we made it up to the second floor, where I dropped to my knees and told her I'd make it the rest of the way without her.

"I won't hear of such a thing," she said, helping me to my feet and letting me lean on her until we reached the bedroom.

"I'll be all right now," I said.

"You're sure?" she asked.

"Yeah," I said. "I'm supposed to bathe my wounds every two hours, but that can wait til morning."

"And risk infection? Nonsense!"

"I don't know what we're gonna do about it," I said. "If I can't give you a friendly little pinch, I hardly figger I can take my clothes off in front of you." I paused for a moment. "Of course, I could turn the lights out and have you swab my wounds in the dark."

"Well..." she said hesitantly, "I *suppose* that would be all right. After all, they *do* have to be cleaned."

Modesty and a sense of literary decorum forbids me from relating the rest of the scene, except to say that after she couldn't find no wounds on me I started pointing out where they were on her so she would have a firmer grasp of the situation, and pretty soon we were grasping each other so firmly that both of us plumb forgot about my wounds, and we might have stayed like that forever except that about four in the morning I woke up and started feeling kind of eleven o'clockish a good seven hours early, so I climbed back into my clothes and moseyed on down to the kitchen to see if I could scare up a little snack, and ran smack dab into General Gruenwald and Lord Mayor Rembert, who were there sipping glasses of brandy.

"You took an enormous risk," said the General. "You should never be alone with anyone who knows Philbert."

"There are certain circumstances under which three is a crowd," I answered. "Or at least a mighty peculiar arrangement."

"Has she guessed who you are yet?"

"No," I said. "But Von Sykoff has. Or, at least, he's guessed who I ain't."

"Damn!" muttered the General. "We'd better triple the guard around Philbert. If Von Sykoff can't get to him, he'll have to come after you."

"Me?"

The General nodded. "Absolutely."

"I don't know how to tell you this gently," I said, "but from my particular point of view, that ain't a consummation devoutly to be wished."

"One can't always have what one wants," said the General.

Well, as you can imagine, I wasn't in no mood to sleep after this particular conversation, and Griselda was in no mood to wake up, so I finally took to wandering through the palace, absently pocketing such little *objets d'art* as caught my eye.

By sun-up the palace was bustling with activity, and I grabbed some breakfast, and then I figured it was time to wake Griselda and send her home, so I went up to the bedroom, but she had other ideas, most of which I'd given her the night before, and it was another hour before I made it back downstairs, where the General and the Lord Mayor were waiting for me.

"It's time for you to make a speech to Parliament," said the Lord Mayor.

"What about?" I asked.

"The economy," said the General. "We've written it down for you. All you have to do is read it."

It sounded easy enough, so I took a quick look at it while we were driving over to the Parliament building, and then, after waiting in the wings to be introduced, I walked up behind a podium and started reading it, but when I came to the part about how we were going to raise the peasants' taxes again I got a better idea, so I just put the speech aside and suggested that maybe we should just let Wilhelm Von Sykoff and his cronies pay for the government, since they were trying to steal it anyway, and suddenly Von Sykoff was on his feet cursing a blue streak and demanding satisfaction, and I explained as patiently as I could that if he hadn't gotten no satisfaction last night I felt right sorry for him, but we didn't want to hear about his sexual problems on the floor of the Parliament.

Then he walked up to the podium and took his glove off and kind of waved it at my face, so I took it from him and tried it on, and explained it was a mite large for me and did he have anything in the next smaller size, and suddenly he was cursing again and carrying on something awful, and insisting that we have a duel.

"Some other time," I said. "I'm busy giving this here speech now."

"You *must* face him, Your Majesty," said one of the members of the Parliament.

"I *am* facing him," I said. "I just ain't gonna fight him."

"The honor of Sylvania demands it," said another.
"He's no Sylvanian!" shouted Von Sykoff. "He's an imposter!"
"Don't pay him no never mind," I said. "He's been out in the sun too long."
"Would King Philbert behave like this?" demanded Von Sykoff.
"He has many faults, but cowardice isn't one of them!"
I turned to General Gruenwald, who was still standing beside me.
"What happens if I admit he's telling the truth?" I whispered.
"You lose the quarter million, and the mob tears you apart."
"And if I don't admit it?"
"Then you have to accept his challenge."
"What weapons is he good with?" I asked.
"All of them."
"Let me reword that just a bit," I said. "Is there anything he *ain't* good at?"
"Losing," said the General.

Well, I figured as long as I was probably going to die anyway, I might just as well die fighting for a quarter of a million dollars, so I turned back to Von Sykoff and said, "Okay, if you want a fight, you got one."

Everyone stood up and cheered, and Von Sykoff just grinned at me and bowed.

"I choose swords," he said. "Everyone knows that Philbert is a superb swordsman. If I am wrong, he will make short work of me."

The Lord Mayor stepped between us and turned to me.

"What type of sword do you select, Your Majesty?"

"There are types?" I asked.

"Certainly," said the Lord Mayor. "There are foils, épées, sabres, scimitars, broad's swords…"

I thunk about it for a moment, and I figured that from the sound of it a broad's sword was probably a dinky little weapon that might not draw much blood, and that maybe we could all shake hands and have a drink when the fight was over.

"I choose broad's swords," I said.

There was a gasp from the audience.

"But we haven't used broad's swords this century!" exclaimed Von Sykoff.

"Well, if you want to call the thing off, I got no serious objections," I said.

"No!" he snapped. "Broad's swords it is."

Well, they cleared a huge area in the middle of the floor, and we each took off our fancy coats and rolled up our sleeves, and then two big burly guys walked out with a long box that looked like it weighed a ton, and they set it on the edges of two chairs and took the top off, and there were the two biggest, heaviest swords I ever did see, and I couldn't help but wonder what kind of broads had been able to fight with them.

Von Sykoff walked over, placed both his hands on the handle of one broad's sword, and dragged it away to where he had been standing. I tried to lift the other one and couldn't, and finally the two guys who had carried 'em out gingerly hefted up the point and helped me take it back to where I was supposed to start.

"Are you ready, Wilhelm?" asked the Lord Mayor.

"Ready," muttered Von Sykoff.

"Are you ready, Your Majesty?"

"Ready?" I said. "Hell, I can't even pick the damned thing up."

"It was *his* choice," said Von Sykoff. "He can't back out now."

"I'm afraid he's right, Your Majesty," said the Lord Mayor. "You will begin on the count of three: one, two, three!"

Well, Von Sykoff somehow or other managed to raise his broad's sword over his head while I was still trying to lift mine off the ground, and he kind of staggered over to where I was. I could see he was about to take a mighty big swing with it, so I made one last effort and pulled on the handle with all my might, but the damned sword was so heavy and my hands were sweating so badly that I lost my grip on it and fell backward just as Von Sykoff's sword came down on where I had been.

It hit the marble floor with the loudest *clang!* I ever did hear, and suddenly Von Sykoff shrieked and dropped his sword and fell to his knees.

"I think I broke both my hands!" he said.

He tried to pick his sword up, screamed again, and let go of it.

"Your Majesty is free to administer the *coup de gras* at your leisure," said the Lord Mayor.

"What in the world do I want a cup of grass for?" I asked.

"He meant you may deliver the death blow whenever you wish," said the General.

"I can't even lift my sword," I said. "Besides, the Good Book tells us never to smite a helpless opponent, especially when he's got a lot of friends and relations watching. Why don't you just cart him off to the calaboose and give him a couple of months to think about whether he really wants to kill the King?"

"I haven't broken any law!" protested Von Sykoff.

"Well, there's another alternative," I said agreeably. "We can all hang around here until I figure out how to lift my sword and finish the fight."

"No," said Von Sykoff. "You win."

So they took him away, and everyone cheered, and even his followers figgered I was a pretty nifty King for letting him live, and the General was pleased as all get out and said that he'd make sure that Von Sykoff stayed in jail until Philbert was back in shape, and the Lord Mayor said that things would be so peaceful for the next month that they could announce I had taken a vacation to the Alps and no one would try to overthrow the government, so I could take my money and leave if I was of a mind to.

It was a mighty tempting proposition, but being the noble and decent Christian gentleman I am I just couldn't bring myself to break poor Griselda's heart, so I hung around for another few weeks, and when Philbert finally got back on the job he found himself a mighty changed and friendly fiancée.

As for me, I finally had enough money to build my tabernacle, and I figured it was time to go scout out the proper location for it—and besides, I'd made it almost a month without running into one of the ladies whose sword I'd used, and the Good Book tells us not to press our luck when we're on a winning streak.

3. TREASURE HUNTING

I figured that if I was finally going to settle down and build my tabernacle it made a lot of sense to do it where the weather was pleasant all year around and the people had been sinning for a good long time, so I headed south to Greece to scout out properties.

I wanted something with a nice view, maybe on a hillside or something like that, but all I could find in Athens were a bunch of real old buildings that were falling apart. So I went further out to the countryside, where the buildings weren't a lot newer but the land was cheaper, and finally found myself in a little town called Tinos, overlooking the Aegean Sea. I decided to put off looking for a room until I stopped off at a local bar for a little something to quench my thirst with maybe just enough alcohol in it to whip the tar out of the germs.

I took my glass to a table in the corner and sat down to drink it in peace and quiet, when suddenly a familiar looking figure sat down next to me.

"Well, fancy meeting you here, Doctor Jones!"

"You got me mistook for someone else," I said as soon as I recognized him. "I ain't never heard of no Doctor Jones."

"Nonsense!" he said with a smile. "This is me, Erich Von Horst, you're talking to."

"Every other time I ever talked to you I wound up dead broke and usually in the hoosegow," I said sullenly.

"Let's let bygones be bygones," he said amiably. He signaled for two more drinks. "I'm buying."

"You ain't never bought nothing in your life," I said.

"You mustn't be so bitter, Doctor Jones," he said. "In the end, all it will do is get you an ulcer."

"Why ain't you still back in Africa, cashing in on elephants' graveyards and lost diamond mines and the like?" I asked.

"Because I found something better here in Greece," he said.

"Well, I wish you luck with it, and don't call me, I'll call you," I said.

"Is that any way to speak to an old friend?" asked Von Horst with a hurt expression on his face.

"Show me an old friend and I'll think about it," I said.

"I see you still have your delightful sense of humor."

"Look," I said. "The first time I laid eyes on you you robbed me of two thousand pounds in Dar es Salaam."

"I paid you back," he said.

"With counterfeit money," I said. "That was the time we met in Algeria."

"You *did* try to swindle me out of the Jacobean Red Letter edition of the Bible," he pointed out.

"There ain't no such thing as a Jacobean Red Letter edition of the Bible!" I shouted at him.

"Ah, but you didn't know it when you tried to cheat me out of it."

"All I know is you wound up with the biggest ruby in Africa and I wound up with a bunch of money that wasn't worth the paper it was writ on!"

"That's all in the past," said Von Horst with a shrug. "I'm a changed man. I'll be happy to make amends."

"I'll just bet," I said.

"If you'd like, we can go to my hotel room just as soon as we've slaked our thirst, and I'll pay you the seven thousand pounds I owe you—the two thousand from Dar es Salaam and the five thousand from Algeria."

"Fine," I said, as the waiter brought us our drinks. "And in the meantime, don't say a word."

"Why on earth not?" he asked.

"Because every time I listen to you it costs me money."

"Doctor Jones, you cut me to the quick!"

"It's a pretty tempting thought," I said.

"Truly, you misjudge me," said Von Horst. "I wish there was some way to make amends for all the trouble I seem to have caused you."

"Just give me my money and get out of my life, and we'll call it square," I said.

"I said I would, and I will," replied Von Horst. He peered across the table at me. "Have *you* got any money?"

"That's none of your business."

He grinned. "*That* much?"

"I don't want to hear this," I said.

"Forget the seven thousand pounds, Doctor Jones," he said. "How would you like to make some *real* money?"

"With you?" I asked.

"Yes."

"I'd hate it."

"You could triple your investment in a week."

"You want me to start quoting psalms at you," I asked, "or should I just hold up a cross to make you go away?"

"There's absolutely no risk involved."

"Go away."

"I just want to make amends for our prior misunderstandings," he said.

"Shut up," I said.

He shrugged. "As you wish."

I finished my drink and sat there staring at my glass for a few minutes.

"I could triple my money in a week?" I said at last.

"At the very least."

"I don't want to hear about it," I said. "Just leave me alone."

"Certainly," he said.

I lit a cigarette and smoked it all the way down.

"No risk?" I said.

"None at all."

"Then what do you need *me* for?"

"I don't," he said. "I'm simply trying to make restitution for my past indiscretions."

"Let's hear it," I said.

"Not here," said Von Horst. "Too many interested ears are listening. Let's go back to my hotel, and I'll lay it out for you."

He got up and I followed him out.

"Beautiful place, Greece," he said as we walked down the pavement. "Far more opportunities for entrepreneurs like you and me than there were in Africa, eh, Doctor Jones?"

"You seemed to find more than your share in Africa," I said.

"Do I detect a trace of bitterness?" he said.

"Von Horst, I trust you about as far as I can spit with my mouth closed," I said. "I'll listen to you until I spot your scam, and then I'm taking my seven thousand pounds and leaving."

"That's all that I ask, Doctor Jones," he said. "By the way, since we're such old friends, may I call you Lucifer?"

"No."

"As you wish," he said with a sigh. "But after I explain this deal to you, you're going to realize that I'm truly doing you an enormous favor."

"The next favor you do anyone will be the first," I said. "Let's just get this over with."

"Ah, here we are," he said, stopping in front of a little waterfront hotel.

"You're making seven thousand an afternoon and you're staying *here*?" I asked.

"I don't want to attract undue attention to myself," he said. "Come on in."

He waved to the desk clerk, and we climbed up to the fourth floor, where he opened a door and led me into a suite of rooms.

"I've rented the entire floor," he said. "Have a seat, Doctor Jones. Can I get you something to drink?"

"Not a thing," I answered him. "Just say what you've got to say and then fork over my money."

"All right," he said, sitting down on a sofa and lighting a thin cigar. "Look out the window and tell me what you see."

"The Aegean Sea," I said.

"Wrong, Doctor Jones," he said enthusiastically. "It's a bank, and there's no door on the vault."

"What the hell are you talking about?" I said.

"I'm saying that we're in similar lines of business these days, Doctor Jones," he replied. "You're in salvation, and I'm in salvage."

"I don't think I follow you."

"You save souls. I save treasures."

"Treasures?" I repeated.

"Do you know how many ships lay beneath that calm surface, Doctor Jones?"

"A few," I said.

"*Hundreds!*" he said, leaning forward. "Warships, trading ships, pirate ships. The treasure they carry runs into *billions!*" He walked over to a desk, took a diamond necklace out of the top drawer, and tossed it to me. "I picked this up yesterday morning. Take a good look at it."

"It looks real," I said.

"It *is* real!"

"Okay," I said. "It's real. So you're a rich man. So what do you need *me* for?"

"It's not that simple," he said with a heavy sigh.

"Somehow it never is," I said.

"Let me lay the situation out for you," he said. "I came here with a lot of money to invest. Some fool bought the elephants' graveyard from me"—I decided not to tell him that the fool was my former partner, Colonel Carcosa, who was probably still gathering dust in a Mozambique jail—"and I was seriously considering retiring. Then I heard about Mazarati's map."

"Mazarati's map?" I asked.

"Enrico Mazarati, a nineteenth-century Italian sailor, spent his entire adult life making a map that marked the location of every wrecked ship in the Aegean, going back to Pericles' time. At first I thought it was a myth, but it piqued my curiosity, and the more I looked into it, the more I became convinced that the map existed. It took me almost five years to hunt it down, and it took every penny I had to purchase it—but it's *mine* now! In the two months I've had it, you wouldn't believe what I've pulled out of the sea!"

"I repeat: what do you need *me* for?"

"Well, there's a little problem with the authorities," he said. "They seem to believe that anything taken out of the Aegean belongs to them, whereas I personally have always believed that possession is one hundred percent of the law."

"Not totally unreasonable," I allowed.

"Since I haven't been able to win them over to my position, I am unable to sell the treasures I've accumulated until such time as I can…ah…*covertly* remove them from the country," continued Von Horst. "I'm finding more every day, but given the situation, my cash flow isn't quite what it should be."

"You're broke," I said.

"Well, not entirely," he replied. "I can afford my rooms at the hotel, and I have a small boat—but with a major infusion of capital,

I could hire the best boat and equipment for the job, and pull these treasures up by the carload rather than one at a time." He looked at me. "Do you see where this is leading?"

"Let me see the map," I said.

He walked over to a painting of a seascape that was hanging on the wall, turned it over, and there, taped to the back of it, was Enrico Mazarati's map, showing the exact locations of maybe four hundred sunken ships.

"How do I know this isn't just another scam?" I asked.

"I show you Mazarati's map and you *still* distrust me?" he demanded.

"Anyone can draw up a map," I said.

"Take the necklace to any jeweler in town and have it evaluated," he said. "If it's not legitimate, I'll pay you double what I owe you and never darken your door again."

"Let's leave it at that," I said, getting up and stuffing the necklace in my pocket. "I'll take it around in the morning, and if it's legit, I'll be back here at noon."

"Fine," he said, standing up and walking me to the door. "Once you find out what it's worth, I'm sure you will be tempted to take it and simply leave the country. If you do that, two things will happen: first, I will inform the authorities that you have stolen a priceless relic belonging to the Greek government, and second, you will not be allowed to share in the vast treasure that I've yet to recover."

"What a thing to suggest about a man of the cloth!" I said, working up a good head of outrage and wondering how he'd figured out my plans so fast.

I found myself a nice old rooming house with lots of character, and the more I thought about it, the more I decided that future generations of tourists would never forgive me if I gave them enough money to cover those beautiful old stucco walls with ugly looking wallpaper, so I kind of tiptoed out while the desk clerk was on the phone, and then I took Von Horst's necklace up the street to the first jeweler I could find.

The man looked at it, then blinked a couple of times, looked again, and offered me ten thousand dollars if I could prove I was the owner. I thanked him for his time, told him I'd consider it, and then, because I knew just how sly Von Horst was, I took it to three other jewelers, just in case he'd paid a couple of 'em off. Every one of them assured me that it was authentic.

This wasn't exactly what I had expected to hear, and it put a whole new light on things. Obviously the Mazarati map was the pure quill, and Von Horst would never have trusted me with real diamonds if he hadn't been sure I'd come back...which meant that he really did have a cash flow problem.

And suddenly I saw a way to make enough money to put me and God on Easy Street while paying Erich Von Horst back for all them times he'd duped me back in Africa.

My mind made up, I grabbed some breakfast, waited until noontime, and moseyed over to his hotel.

"Well?" he said.

"It's real," I said, handing the necklace back to him.

"Are you in or out?" he asked.

"In," I said.

"Excellent," he said, shaking my hand. "We'll begin this afternoon."

"Well, we got a little problem there," I said. "My money ain't where I can lay my hands on it. It'll take me a couple of days to move it to Tinos."

He frowned. "I hate to wait," he said. "Every day we sit here is another day that someone else might discover some of the treasure. How much money are we talking about?"

"Maybe a quarter of a million," I said.

"Pounds?"

"Dollars."

"That's fabulous!" he exclaimed. "For that kind of money, we can buy every boat in Tinos. We'll lock the competition out!"

"They can always go to some other town and buy boats," I said.

"By the time they do that and get back here, we'll have pulled up the treasure from all the nearby wrecks," replied Von Horst, "and without the Mazarati map they'll never find the rest...and that alone will pay for the boats twenty times over."

"Sounds good to me," I said.

"In the meantime," he added, "there's no reason why we shouldn't pull a quick ten or twenty thousand dollars out of the sea this afternoon. I've got until sundown on the boat I've been using before the lease runs out."

"Sounds good to me," I said. "Just give me some time to send for the money."

"Fine," he said. "I'll meet you at the docks in, shall we say, an hour?"

"Make it two, just to be on the safe side," I said.

The first thing I did when I left his hotel was go to a local map shop and buy a map of the area just about the same size as the Mazarati map. Then I took it to the library, where no one would bother me, and traced it onto a sheet of blank paper I had bought, so it would look like the authentic Mazarati map. Finally, I marked about four hundred shipwreck locations, just making little X's like the Mazarati map had done. When I was through, I threw the original map into the garbage and folded up the map I'd just made and stuck it into one of my pockets. Then I went to the dustiest, emptiest section of the library, pulled out my wad of money, and stuck it behind a huge copy of *Eighteenth Century British Maritime Rules and Regulations*, which looked like it hadn't been touched since Queen Victoria was in bloomers.

I checked with the head librarian on the way out and found that the place was open until six o'clock. Then I went on down to the docks, where I found Von Horst waiting for me by a beat-up fishing boat with a motor that looked like it had seen a lifetime's worth of better days.

"*This* is what we're going out in?" I asked.

"It's seaworthy, and it doesn't attract attention," he said. "I've got the diving gear hidden under the canvas." He tossed me a fishing rod. "Here. Let people see you holding this so they think we're just a pair of tourists going out for a little sport."

Well, I spent a couple of minutes playing with the rod for the benefit of any onlookers, and then we hopped into the boat and Von Horst started the motor, and when we were maybe a mile off the shore he pulled out his map and checked his compass, then turned about two hundred yards to his left.

"We should be right over the wreck of the *Isadora*," he said.

"Never heard of it."

"It's an old Spanish galleon that theoretically carried grain and fabrics, but actually trafficked in stolen gemstones." He pulled back the canvas to reveal a deepsea diving suit. "I'm afraid all I could afford was one. We'll take turns using it. You can go first."

"Me?" I said. "I ain't never been in nothing like that. How do I breathe?"

"The same as always," he said. "I'll pump the air while you're beneath the surface."

"Just a minute," I said. "Who pumped the air for you before I showed up?"

"A lovely young lady of my acquaintance who thought we were looking for shells," he said. "The diving outfit was too heavy for her to manipulate, so she never dove down and hence never knew about all the sunken ships."

I climbed into the deepsea suit, and as Von Horst was adjusting my helmet, I said, "You realize that if you stop pumping air, two things are gonna happen: first, I'm gonna die, and second, you ain't never gonna see a penny of that quarter million."

"I swear I never met such a distrustful man," he said.

Well, he lowered me down, and I turned on the light at the top of my helmet. There were enough fish to feed the whole of Hong Kong with maybe enough left over for Tokyo, but finally they cleared away and suddenly I could see this old, rotting Spanish ship. It took a while to learn how to maneuver, but eventually I landed on the deck, and walked into a couple of the rooms, which didn't have nothing in them except old rotting furniture.

But when I hit the third room, I tried the top drawer of a dresser that hadn't rotted apart yet, and inside it was a bunch of bright, glittery stuff. I picked it up, stuck it in a pouch on my outfit, walked back out to the deck, and signaled that I wanted Von Horst to pull me up.

"Did you find anything?" he asked when I was finally back on the boat.

I reached into my pouch and pulled out one of the objects.

"A diamond tiara!" he said. "Fit for a queen—or a reputable fence. What else do you have?"

I emptied the pouch, and we counted up two sets of diamond earrings and a pearl necklace.

"Not bad, partner," he said. "Did you ransack the whole boat?"

"I just tried three or four cabins," I said. "There must be fifty of 'em."

"I think I'll go down and have a look for myself," he said. "If you don't mind climbing out of the suit."

It took about ten minutes for me to get out of the outfit and him to get back in, and then he was down inspecting the ship and I was pumping air to him. I figured an experienced treasure hunter like him would stay down half an hour or so, but less than a minute later he jerked on the line, the signal that he wanted to come up. I hauled him to the surface, and then, just before dragging him up out of the water and onto the deck, I took the phony map out of my pocket and substituted it for the Mazarati map, which I removed from his coat and tucked inside my shirt.

"That was mighty fast," I said.

"Sharks," he said, removing the helmet and starting to climb out of the outfit. "One of them looked like he was thinking of biting right through the air hose."

"Well, we made a pretty decent haul anyway," I said. "I suppose we can come back when my money arrives."

"Still," he said, "it seems a shame to waste the rest of the afternoon. I can find another location on the map."

"It ain't necessary," I said.

"It's no problem," he insisted. "The map's right here."

"I'm all tuckered out," I said, since I didn't want him doing no close inspection of the map. "I ain't used to walking around underwater like unto a fish."

"You're sure?" he said, walking over to his jacket. "It's no trouble to find another ship."

I grabbed my stomach and moaned. "I think I'm getting a case of the folds."

"You mean the bends?"

"Whatever," I moaned. "Let's just pack it in and go on home."

"Whatever you say," replied Von Horst, turning his attention from the map to the engine, and about half an hour later we were parked at one of the docks.

"How are you feeling?" he asked when we got back on dry land.

"Better," I said.

"If you're up to dinner, we'll celebrate today's finds with the best meal in town. My treat."

"I don't think I could look at food tonight," I said. "I'll just go back to my room and lay down. I should be fit again by the morning."

"Take all the time you need to recuperate," he said. "As long as your money won't arrive for a couple of days, and my lease on the boat has run out, you might as well spend tomorrow in bed regaining your strength. I'll meet you the day after tomorrow."

"Sounds good to me," I said.

"Take care now," he said. "I'd hate to lose you before the money arrives."

Well, that sounded like the Von Horst I knew, so I bade him good bye and started staggering off, with the Mazarati map, the tiara, the necklace, and the earrings all safely tucked away on various parts of my person. When I was sure I was out of sight, I straightened up and resumed my normal gait and rushed over to the library, where I retrieved my money.

Then, while Von Horst ate his fancy dinner and went back to his suite to relax, I went down to the docks and bought every boat in town. Most of the here sailors and fishermen drove mighty hard bargains, but by dawn I owned every boat in Tinos and still had about two thousand dollars left, which as far as I could see left Von Horst out in the cold and made me the sole owner of the treasures on Mazarati's map.

Then, bright and early the next morning, while Von Horst was still asleep, I went down to the docks, found the boat Von Horst had leased, and hired a little Greek feller to pump my air for me. I pulled out Mazarati's map, pinpointed the *Isadora*, and steered the boat until we were directly over it. Then I changed into the deepsea gear and went down to find some treasure.

Well, I must have spent three hours going over the *Isadora*, and I couldn't find so much as a tie pin. Finally I went back up to the surface and took the boat back to shore, where I figured on having lunch before setting out to spend the afternoon going over the rest of the *Isadora*.

I was sitting down eating a sandwich in a little *taverna* when a heavyset, bearded feller who smelled of fish walked up to me.

"You are Lucifer Jones, are you not?" he asked.

"The Right Reverend Lucifer Jones at your service," I said.

He pulled up a chair and sat down across the table from me. "I wonder if you could answer a question, Reverend Jones," he said.

"If it's within my power, I'd be right happy to, Brother," I said. "What particular question did you have in mind?"

"What is so valuable about our boats that you paid so much for the entire fleet?"

"Let's just say I'm a kind of collector," I told him.

He leaned back and scratched his head. "I didn't know anyone collected old fishing boats," he said. "I guess Mr. Von Horst was right."

"Von Horst?" I said. "What's he got to do with anything?"

"When he bought our fleet two days ago, he told us that if we were patient, a collector would come by sometime within the next week and buy the whole fleet for at least ten times what he paid for it."

"But I didn't buy the boats from *him*," I said, with that old familiar sinking feeling in the pit of my stomach. "I bought 'em from *you* guys."

"Oh, no," he corrected me. "They have been Mr. Von Horst's boats for two days. But he was very generous: he paid us each a fifteen percent commission to sell them for him."

"Where is he now?" I demanded.

The man shrugged. "I don't know. He collected his money while you were out fishing this morning, and that was the last I saw of him."

I raced out of the restaurant and didn't stop until I came to a jeweler, one of the few I hadn't visited with the diamond necklace the day before.

"Quick," I said, slapping the tiara, the earrings, and the pearls down on the counter. "What are these worth?"

He just looked at them without even putting on his little eyepiece, and then turned to me. "The same thing they were worth when I sold them to Mr. Von Horst last week," he said. "About three dollars. Well, make that two—they almost look like someone has been keeping them in salt water. See how the gold paint is pitted here?"

"You mean you only deal in costume jewelry?" I demanded.

"Of course not," he replied. "I deal in whatever the market will bear. In fact, if you'd like a truly beautiful piece of authentic jewelry, perhaps I can interest you in this diamond necklace that Mr. Von Horst just returned after renting for a week."

He held up the same necklace I'd had appraised the day before, and I screamed a couple of things I hoped my Silent Partner didn't overhear, and rushed off to Von Horst's hotel. As I was heading to the stairway, the desk clerk looked up and called over to me.

"Doctor Jones?"

"Yeah?"

"I'm afraid your friend has checked out. Something about an illness in the family. He left you this note."

I walked over to the desk, opened the envelope, and read as follows:

My dear Doctor Jones:

How very fortuitous it was to meet you once again. Very few people, having been burnt once, will willingly stick their hands in the fire a second time, and yet here you are, after three unfortunate experiences on the Dark Continent, once again attempting to swindle me.

Still, some people are slower learners than others, and while I was not waiting specifically for you, you can imagine my surprise and delight when you showed up in the bar the other night.

By now you have doubtless figured out that there never was an Enrico Mazarati. He is one of my, shall we say, business names, and I hereby will him to you, along with the map that took me the better part of an afternoon to draw. (It won't do you much good, alas; I have been assured that the Isadora is the only wreck within fifty miles of here.) Nor are there any sharks in the vicinity; I knew you couldn't switch maps while you were pumping air, so I decided that the sooner I came back to the surface, the sooner you would be free to steal my map and begin bringing this affair to a satisfactory conclusion.

Still, you might look at the bright side: you are now the commander of your very own fishing fleet. I trust this pleases you, as I am afraid you are stuck with it, since you paid approximately one thousand percent of market value for the boats, and the commissions I handed out this morning have all been earmarked for new boats.

Oh, and keep the pearls and the tiara: there's always a chance you may run into a young lady who is as greedy and gullible as you yourself are.

Yr. Obdt. Svt.,

Erich Von Horst

Five seconds later I got a case of the bends.

4. THE LOST CONTINENT

After my unfortunate treasure-hunting experience off the coast of Tinos, I decided to head back to Athens. I couldn't see no sense purchasing a first-class compartment that might better go to visiting royalty, assuming any such was in the area and hankering for a night on the town in Athens, so I moseyed up the track about a mile, figuring to hop a lift in a freight car and save the price of a ticket.

Well, it turns out that I wasn't the only guy with that idea, because I found an old feller sitting next to a small fire, warming up a cup of coffee in an empty tin can.

"Howdy," I said. "You mind if I join you?"

"Help yourself," he said in perfect American. "You sound like a countryman."

"The Right Reverend Doctor Lucifer Jones at your service," I said, shaking his gnarly old hand.

"Pleased to meet you," he said. "I'm Zachariah MacDonald, from West Allis, Wisconsin."

"We're practically neighbors," I said. "I hail from Moline, Illinois—though I ain't been back there, or even to America, in many a year."

"Me neither," said MacDonald. "What are you doing here in Tinos?"

"Mostly looking for a way out," I said.

"I mean, what are you doing abroad in the first place?" he asked.

"I heard the siren song of romance, mystery and adventure," I said. "As well as the footsteps of various biased and misguided prosecuting attorneys coming up behind me."

"Where are you off to?" he asked.

"Oh, it don't make much difference," I said. "Athens seems as good a place as any."

"You don't sound wildly enthused," said MacDonald.

"One place is pretty much like another," I said. "It all depends on the opportunities."

"Now there we disagree," he said. "I find all places absolutely unique and different from each other. For example, have you ever been to Africa?"

"Yeah, I spent a few years there."

"And you've no desire to go back?"

"Desire ain't got nothing to do with it," I said. "I been invited to keep off that particular land mass due to a series of innocent misunderstandings by the local authorities."

"How about Asia?"

"Same problem," I admitted.

"Can you go back to America?"

"Well, I *think* I'm still allowed in Montana and Arkansas," I said.

"It sounds like you've led a most interesting life," he said, backing off just a bit.

"I'm just a God-fearing man of the cloth who's trying to establish a tabernacle and bring the Word of the Lord to all these depraved Europeans." I paused. "How about you, Brother Zachariah? What brings a Wisconsin man to this here forsaken little spot in the Greek countryside?"

"The culmination of my life's work," he said.

"You been working all your life just to sit here and hop a freight for Athens?" I asked.

He shook his head. "Of course not."

"Well, then?"

"I was a professor of geology at the University of Wisconsin for close to thirty years," said MacDonald. "My special field of study was lost continents: Lemuria, Mu, Gondwanaland, and the like."

"Yeah?"

He nodded. "Most of them are myths, of course—but about twenty years ago I became convinced, from certain hints both in

Plato and elsewhere, that Atlantis actually existed, that it was not merely a myth."

"And you think it's somewhere near this here railroad track?" I asked.

"No, of course not. Over the years I pieced together every bit of data I could get my hands on. Then, when I was sure I was right, I quit my job, cashed in my life savings, and went hunting for it." Suddenly he smiled triumphantly. "And four months ago I found it!"

"Funny how that little piece of news didn't make the papers," I said.

"I haven't made it public yet," he said. "There are others who are also searching for it, who would gladly kill me if they knew I had found it first. I'm on my way to stake my claim right now."

"If you can't afford to buy a ticket on the train," I said, "how do you figure you to pay for a whole lost continent?"

"Oh, I've got the money," he said. "It's safely tucked away in a bank in Athens. But my competitors—no Cretins, they—have finally figured out that I found what I was looking for, and there have been a series of attempts on my life. I'd have been a sitting duck at the Tinos train station."

"Well, if they know that Atlantis is near Tinos, ain't they likely to buy it out from under you anyway?" I asked.

"It's nowhere near here. I've been in Tinos for a month to throw them off the scent." He frowned. "The problem is, I did *too* good a job of it. I convinced them so thoroughly that it's near Tinos that they now feel free to kill me." Suddenly he stared at me. "You seem like a man of action, Doctor Jones. How would you like to hire on as my bodyguard?"

"Well, the Tabernacle of Saint Luke *is* a mite short of funds these days," I allowed. "What's the job pay?"

"Five thousand dollars, for a week's work."

"Brother Zachariah," I said, "you got yourself a bodyguard."

"Excellent!" he said, shaking on it. "By the way, I don't believe I've ever heard of the Tabernacle of Saint Luke."

"Well, it ain't real well established around these here parts," I admitted.

"In fact," he continued, "I'm not aware of *any* church or tabernacle named after Saint Luke."

"Well, it seemed more modest that calling it the Tabernacle of Saint Lucifer," I said, "me not yet having been canonized or nothing."

"You're a very enterprising young man," he said.

"Well, the Lord teaches us to grab what's there."

"He does?"

"I practice an exceptionally aggressive form of Christianity," I explained.

"Where did you learn it?" he asked.

"Oh, it's just something me and the Lord worked out betwixt ourselves of a Sunday afternoon back in Moline," I replied. "So far it's served me pretty well, except for them occasions when it hasn't."

Well, we chatted for a few more minutes, and then the train came along, and we hopped into a open cattle car and slid the door shut. The train stopped at Tinos for about five minutes, no one looked into our car, and then we took off again, hitting Athens about six hours later.

We waited til the station was pretty much deserted, then caught a cab and went straight to the Grande Bretagne Hotel, where MacDonald had an account, and they gave us a pair of connecting rooms on the sixth floor, overlooking Constitution Square. He was afraid to go down to the restaurant, so we had room service deliver us a dinner of *dolmades* and *mousaka* and *pastitso* and *saganaki* and all kinds of pastries, and by the time we were done I was wondering why I hadn't discovered the bodyguard business a long time ago.

Then a shot rang out and the window shattered and we both hit the floor, and I realized that there was more to bodyguarding than met the eye.

"Get out your gun!" he whispered.

"I don't know quite how to tell you this, Brother Zachariah," I said, "but I ain't got no gun."

"What kind of bodyguard are you?" he snapped.

"Right now I'm concentrating real hard on being a live one," I said. "Beyond that, I ain't too particular at this here point in time."

"Did you at least see where the shot came from?" he asked.

"Well, if it didn't come from outside, we're in a lot more trouble than I hope we are," I answered.

"What use are you?" he demanded.

"Well, I never claimed to be a bodyguard by trade," I said. "On the other hand, if they manage to kill you, I'll give you the best send-off any funeral's ever seen."

"Let's crawl to the door," he said. "We'll be safer in the corridor."

I didn't necessarily agree with that, since I didn't know who might be waiting in the corridor to greet us, but then another shot came through the window and we high-tailed it to the door and raced out of the room. The corridor was empty, and we decided that trying to leave the hotel wouldn't be the brightest course of action, since someone on the outside already knew we were there, so instead we climbed down to the third floor and found a real small broom closet without no windows.

"I'll wait here," said MacDonald. "You go down to the desk and have them phone the police."

That didn't have no more appeal to me than returning to the room to finish up the pastries.

"Maybe you'd better go, Brother Zachariah," I said. "I don't speak Greek."

"The desk clerk speaks English."

"He'd probably be more inclined to believe a regular customer of good standing in the community," I said.

"Just *do* it!" he said, shoving me out into the corridor and locking the door behind me.

Well, I couldn't see no point to standing out there all night, so I walked over to the elevator and pushed the button, and a minute later I was down on the main floor, walking over to the desk, when a couple of well-dressed gentlemen walked over and grabbed me by each arm and escorted me out the door and to a black car that was waiting at the curb. Then they frisked me and had me climb into the back seat between them.

"What is your name?" demanded the taller one, shoving a pistol into my short ribs.

"The Honorable Right Reverend Doctor Lucifer Jones at your service," I said.

"I hope so," he said.

"Just check my passport if you doubt me, Brother."

"I meant that I hope you will be at our service," he said. "What is your exact relationship to Professor Zachariah MacDonald?"

"I'm kind of a paid traveling companion," I said.

"Enough talk!" snapped the shorter man. "Has he found it?"

"Has *who* found *what*?" I asked.

"You know precisely what I'm talking about: has MacDonald found what he's been looking for?"

"Last I saw of him, he was mostly looking for a place to hide," I said.

"Listen to me, Reverend Jones," said the taller one. "I don't know what your involvement is, but whatever he's paying you, we'll triple it."

"Let me get this straight," I said. "He's paying me five thousand dollars to keep him alive for a week. You're saying that *you'll* pay me fifteen thousand to keep him alive?"

"Don't play the fool with me, Reverend Jones!" said the taller man. "We'll pay you fifteen thousand to come over to our side."

"You want me to protect *you* from *him*?"

I thunk the tall guy was going to hit me with his gun, but the short one reached over and stopped him.

"What he means, Reverend Jones," he said, pronouncing each word real slow and careful-like, "is that we will pay you to keep us informed of Professor MacDonald's plans—and if you can tell us where Atlantis is before he stakes his claim and makes the news public, we'll pay you a bonus of another fifteen thousand."

"Well, that seems right generous," I said. "But you got to promise me that you won't kill him."

"Why not?" demanded the tall guy.

"He's paying me to keep him alive," I explained. "That would be a breach of faith."

"But telling us his plans isn't?" he asked, surprised.

"He just hired me to guard his body, not his secrets," I said. "Have we got a deal?"

The two looked at each other, and then nodded.

"What are your names, and how do I contact you?" I asked them.

"You may call us Mr. Tall and Mr. Short, and we'll contact *you*," said Mr. Short. "From this moment on, you'll never be out of our sight."

They opened the door and sent me back into the hotel. I didn't see much sense stopping at the broom closet to tell MacDonald that the coast was clear, since he was bound to ask why, and I figured he wouldn't see the situation quite the same way I did, so I went up to his room, finished off the *baklava* and a bottle of *ouzo*, and then sacked out in my own room right next door.

When I woke up I checked the clock and saw it was about noontime, so I opened the connecting door to MacDonald's room to see if he was ready to go to the bank yet, but he wasn't nowhere to be seen. I went down to the lobby looking for him, but although Mr. Tall and Mr. Short were there waiting for us, the desk clerk told me that MacDonald hadn't come down yet.

I figured the only place left that he could possibly be was the broom closet on the third floor, so I went up there to open it, and found it was still locked.

"Come on, Brother Zachariah!" I shouted, pounding away on the door. "It's almost noon. You can't stay in there forever."

Well, I must have kept it up for a good ten minutes with no answer, and suddenly Mr. Tall and Mr. Short were standing beside me, and finally Mr. Tall pulled out a little piece of wire and picked the lock and opened the door, and there was poor Zachariah Mac-Donald, sprawled out on the floor.

"Dead?" asked Mr. Short.

Mr. Tall felt for a pulse. "Definitely. It must have been all these ammonia fumes in a closed room."

Which brought my one and only attempt at bodyguarding to a sorry end.

"Well, Doctor Jones," said Mr. Short, "you're working exclusively for us now. We won't pay you the fifteen thousand for telling us the dear departed's plans, of course, but we'll pay you the other fifteen if you can figure out where Atlantis is."

"In the meantime," said Mr. Long, "let's carry poor Professor MacDonald up to his room so that he doesn't disturb the hotel guests, and we can go over his pockets and such without any untimely interruptions."

Well, the three of us didn't have much trouble carting Brother Zachariah, who wasn't all that big or tall, up to his room, where Mr. Tall and Mr. Short stripped him down to the buff looking for clues.

"Damn!" said Mr. Tall when they were done. "There's nothing but his bank book—and now that he's dead, that won't do us any good."

"Did he have any luggage, Reverend Jones?" asked Mr. Short.

"Not a thing," I said. "He was traveling just as light as I was."

"*Think*, Reverend Jones!" said Mr. Tall. "Did he say anything, anything at all, that might give you a hint as to where Atlantis is?"

"Nothing. Just that it wasn't nowhere near Tinos, that he'd wasted a month there to throw you off the trail."

"Did he tell you where he'd been before going to Tinos?"

"Not as I recall."

"Then that son of a dog died with the secret intact!" said Mr. Tall.

"Hey, that's no way to speak of the dead," I said. "Especially since he always spoke kindly of you."

"He did?" said Mr. Short sharply. "I thought he held all competitors in complete contempt. *What* did he say?"

"He allowed as to how you were pretty bright fellers."

"That hardly sounds like MacDonald," said Mr. Short.

"Maybe not," I said. "But he kept saying that you weren't no Cretins."

"That's *it*!" screamed Mr. Short.

"What are you talking about?" I asked.

"He didn't say Cretin!" said Mr. Short. "He said Cretan! It was his way of having a little joke!"

"I don't follow you," I said.

"He found Atlantis off the coast of Crete!" exclaimed Mr. Short excitedly. "And when he said that we were not Cretans, he meant that we could never be expected to find it!"

"It makes sense," agreed Mr. Tall, studying the bank book. "His bank has a branch on Crete, and that's where he made his last two transactions."

"So all we have to do is buy the submerged land around Crete and we'll be rich beyond our wildest dreams!" said Mr. Short.

"Excuse me for interrupting," I said, "but getting rich beyond my wildest dreams is one of my favorite conversational subjects. What has Atlantis got that makes it so valuable?"

"Artifacts from a civilization that existed a millennium before Christ!" said Mr. Tall. "Artifacts that no one has ever seen before. By the time we finish selling them to museums and collectors, we can practically buy our own country!"

"What makes you think the government of Crete is gonna be real anxious to sell it to you?" I asked.

"They won't *know* they're selling us Atlantis," said Mr. Short. "We'll merely buy dredging rights for a few miles in each direction."

"I don't want to sound ungrateful or nothing," I said, "but fifteen thousand dollars seems a small price to pay me for helping you becoming billionaires."

"We're not through doing business with you yet, Reverend Jones," said Mr. Tall.

"No?"

"Unfortunately, Mr. Short and I have had certain…ah…technical disagreements with the authorities on Crete."

"It's true," added Mr. Short. "They would be most unhappy to see us show up there."

"They might even ask how we came by the money we plan to use to purchase Atlantis," chimed in Mr. Tall.

"In fact," said Mr. Short, "there are probably fifty or sixty customers of the Bank of Crete who would be more than happy to tell them."

"It's our own fault for leaving so many witnesses alive," added Mr. Tall, "but how were we to know the bank would be that crowded?"

"We simply didn't have enough bullets for them all," explained Mr. Short. "It was most unprofessional of us, and I assure you it will never happen again."

"But in the meantime," concluded Mr. Tall, "it would probably be best if someone else were to purchase Atlantis—someone totally unknown to the Cretan authorities."

"You're looking at him," I said proudly. "I don't even know where Crete is."

"Fine," said Mr. Tall. "Then it appears that we will be able to do some more business, Reverend Jones."

"I'm all ears," I said.

"We don't know how much money it will take to purchase Atlantis, so we may have a momentary cash flow problem," said Mr. Short. "But if you will forego your fifteen thousand dollars now, we will give you five percent of everything we recover, which should come to considerably more. A thousandfold, at the very minimum."

"Well, that's right generous of you gentlemen," I said. "But if you will allow me an indiscreet question, how can I be sure you'll give me a fair accounting of what you owe me—not that I think for a single moment that you'd ever cheat a partner. View it as an academic question."

Mr. Tall chuckled. "In point of fact, Dr. Jones, it's *we* who have to make sure that *you* don't cheat *us*. Everything will be registered in your name, so all the revenues will come to you."

"Now," added Mr. Short, "can *we* be sure that you'll give *us* a fair accounting of what you owe us?"

"You ask that of a man of the cloth?" I said.

"We'd simply like to hear your reassurances."

"Brother Short," I said, "I wouldn't never cheat no partner. That's contrary to the Seventh and Twelfth Commandments."

"Then we're in business," said Mr. Tall. "Let's stop wasting time here and catch the next plane to Crete."

"What about poor Brother MacDonald?" I asked. "Seems we ought to give him some kind of a send-off, long as he's the one who's making us all rich."

"Well, we'd like to," said Mr. Short uneasily. "But unfortunately, should the Athens police see us at his graveside, they might ask some embarrassing questions."

"That ain't no problem," I said. "I'll vouch that he died by accident."

"Oh, they won't ask about Mr. MacDonald," said Mr. Short. "Not at first, anyway."

"But when they finish asking about the other seventeen misunderstandings, they might well want to know about poor Mr. MacDonald as well," added Mr. Tall.

"Well, the Good Book teaches us to be adaptable, so why don't we all just observe a moment's silence right now?" I suggested.

Which we did.

Then we went down to the black car, which was parked by the curb, and headed out to the airport, where we found that there weren't no scheduled flights to Crete for the next four days, so Mr. Tall chartered us a plane—leastwise, I *think* he chartered it, though the pilot didn't seem none too happy about the proceedings—and a few hours later we landed on Crete.

It was too late in the day to visit the government offices, so we spent the night in the El Greco Hotel, which took in tourists, roaches and rats with equal hospitality, and in the morning we headed on over to the Heraklion Public Works building. Just before we got there, Mr. Small handed me a thick envelope and told me that it contained all the money he figured I'd need for dredging rights, and that he planned on getting a strict accounting the minute I came out.

Well, it took me a good hour and a half to get to the right department, and then another hour to make myself understood, but by noon I was the proud owner to the dredging rights to Atlantis for a mere thirty-two thousand dollars, which was two thousand more than was in the envelope, so I used my last two grand to cover it, and I walked back out carrying the certificate that made it all legal. Then we celebrated with lunch, and in the afternoon Mr. Tall and

Mr. Short hired a mighty impressive-looking boat and we all went out to pull a few rare pots and pans out of the ruins of Atlantis.

We sent down half a dozen divers, all loaded with sacks and pouches to pull up their treasure. What they brung up was three sea shells and a blowfish.

"Where are the artifacts?" demanded Mr. Short.

"I keep telling you," said the captain of the ship, "we have sailed this sea all our lives, and we have never seen a trace of this lost continent or city or whatever it is."

"Maybe we're not looking in the right place," said Mr. Tall. "Let's head south."

The captain shrugged. "It's your money."

Well, we looked south and east and north and west. We looked right off the shore, and twenty miles out to sea, and eighty miles out to sea. We looked halfway to Italy and all the way back to Greece, but after a month we had to conclude that we had guessed wrong: there wasn't no lost continent, or even a lost suburb, off the island of Crete.

"I suppose in every enterprise, there comes a time to pull up stakes and call it a day," said Mr. Short while we were eating dinner at a little waterfront *taverna*.

"That's what happens when you put your faith in an academic," said Mr. Tall distastefully. "Obviously the late lamented Professor MacDonald really *did* mean Cretin, and now the secret of Atlantis has gone to the grave with him."

"We'll head back to the mainland tomorrow morning," said Mr. Short.

"Since you guys are quitting and there ain't no million dollars' worth of old ashtrays and such to be dug up out of the sea," I said, "what about my fifteen thousand dollars?"

"You stood to make a fortune if we had succeeded," said Mr. Tall. "I see no reason why we should bear the brunt of our failure alone."

"Well, at least give me five thousand," I said. "If you guys hadn't been after him, poor Brother Zachariah would have lasted out the week and I'd have earned my bodyguard money."

"Nonsense," said Mr. Short. "You're the legal owner of Atlantis, such as it is. Go sublease the dredging rights."

"That's *it*?" I demanded. "You're just gonna get up and walk away?"

"Well, if you feel we've been unfair to you in any way, we could shoot you first," suggested Mr. Tall.

The conversation kind of flattened out and lay there like a dead fish after that, and the next morning Mr. Tall and Mr. Short were gone, leaving me with nothing but my last fifteen dollars and the ownership of a continent that was so lost nobody could find it.

I figured I might as well head back to the mainland, too, but when I went to the airport I found out that I didn't have enough money to pay for a plane ticket, and they wouldn't extend me no credit even though I was a man of the cloth. Then I moseyed over to the docks, and discovered that there weren't any boats leaving for the next three days.

So since I was stuck there, I got to thinking about what Mr. Short had said about my being the legal owner of Atlantis, and suddenly the Lord hit me between the eyes with one of His better revelations, and I walked over to the telegraph office and got ahold of the biggest newspaper in Athens and spent all but my last seventeen cents placing an ad.

I had given my address as the El Greco Hotel, so I spent my nights sleeping on a park bench and my days hanging around the lobby, and sure enough, in three days the money started pouring in, and within a week I'd made a quick forty-two thousand dollars and had barely scratched the surface of my potential market, and just when it seemed like me and God were finally gonna get our tabernacle, a bunch of Cretan police officers entered the El Greco's lobby and had a quick conversation with the desk clerk, who pointed to me, and a minute later I was being dragged, none too gently, to a squad car, and a couple of minutes after that we pulled up at the police station and they escorted me into a room with a single chair and damp white walls.

"Is anyone gonna tell me what's going on?" I demanded. "I'm a peaceful law abiding businessman what ain't been bothering no one, and suddenly you guys drag me off like I was some kind of undesirable or something."

"You are Lucifer Jones, are you not?" said the captain of the squad.

"The Right Reverend Lucifer Jones," I corrected him.

"The same Lucifer Jones who placed an advertisement last week in *The Daily Athenian*?"

"Yeah, that's me."

"I hate to think of how many laws you have broken, Reverend Jones," said the captain.

I pulled out my certificate of dredging rights. "I stand on the law," I said. "I got every legal right to subdivide what I own and sell it off."

"You do understand, do you not, that every square centimeter of land you own is under the water?"

"So what?"

"Then how can you possibly sell lots with, as the ad says, 'a Mediterranean view'?"

"I didn't never say what angle the view was from," I replied. "*Caviar empire.*"

He shook his head. "I am afraid we will have to confiscate any money you have appropriated and return it to the poor dupes who answered your advertisement," he said. "And of course," he added, taking my certificate away, "your dredging rights have been revoked."

"Then give me my thirty-two thousand dollars and we'll call it square," I said.

"Your fine comes to thirty one thousand nine hundred dollars or fifteen years in jail," he said calmly. "The choice is yours."

Well, I growled and I grumbled, but finally I didn't have no choice but to pay the fine.

"Now give me my hundred dollars and let me out of here," I said.

"First you must sign over all claims to dredging rights," he said. "Then it will be my pleasure to place you on a plane that is leaving for Rome in less than an hour."

"Who do I sign the rights over to?" I asked, looking at the certificate.

He frowned. "The Heraklion Public Works building is closed today. To facilitate matters, you can sign them over to me—Captain Hektor Papadoras—and I will conclude the paperwork tomorrow."

I did what he said, and they put me on the plane—which cost sixty of the hundred dollars they owed me—and a few hours later I was in Rome, chastising my Silent Partner for turning His back on me just when things were going well for the two of us.

I ate something I hadn't never heard of called a pizza pie for dinner, which I decided was okay for Italy but would never catch on in the States, and then I found a cheap hotel and took a room there.

The next morning I picked up a newspaper and read a feature about how an enterprising Cretan policeman named Hektor Papadoras was selling private fishing concessions off the coast of his island.

I gave my Silent Partner a serious talking to, explained that He'd been falling down on the job and that I expected better of Him in the future, and then I set out afresh to make my fortune and bring His word to the degenerate heathen of the Roman Empire, or such portion of it as I could snugly fit in the Tabernacle of Saint Luke once it got itself built.

5. EXERCISING GHOSTS

For a city that all roads were supposed to lead to, Rome wasn't exactly the most dazzling municipality I'd ever encountered. Of course, it may well be that I was somewhat hampered in my ability to enjoy its sights and sounds by the fact that I only had seventeen cents in my pocket, all that remained from my unfortunate ventures into treasure hunting and buying lost continents (which in this case was so lost that nobody ain't found it to this very day).

Still, it takes more than poverty and a string of bad luck to keep a good Christian down, especially a man of the cloth, so I headed on down the Via Veneto looking for some way to replenish my funds, which was when I realized that even though the Vatican was right next door I was surrounded by a bunch of pagans, because even though I hunted up three different craps games on street corners none of the participants was willing to take my marker, even after I explained that I was toiling in the personal service of the Lord.

Never one to be downcast by cruel turns of Fate, I hung around the bus terminal until a batch of Americans got off about noontime, introduced myself as their guide, and collected a quick three dollars a head from all seventeen of 'em. Fortunately they didn't know Rome any better than I did, so nobody objected as I led 'em through town pointing out Buckingham Palace and the Louvre and other such historic sights as I reckoned were towering about the countryside somewhere. It was when I was explaining to them how the Sistine Brothers had hired Leonardo da Vinci to give their chapel a couple of coats of paint that I began to detect unhappy stirrings in my little group, and by the time I got around to trying to collect some more money for a gondola ride to the Tower of Pisa they all just up and left.

Still, fifty-one dollars for two hours of work wasn't bad pay, though it only took me ten minutes to lose it once I scared up another game of chance. I figured my Silent Partner had His attention directed elsewhere for the time being, and I was seriously considering taking a little fling at the guide business when I heard the worst kind of shrieking and wailing coming from a nearby house, and then the door opened and a priest walked out, followed by a pudgy-looking woman.

"I told you this would be a waste of time, Signora," he said. "Probably you need an exterminator."

"I need *you!*" she hollered.

"You are a superstitious old woman," he said. "Your church has more important things to do. You must stop bothering us with these foolish requests."

He turned on his heel and walked away, and she started weeping and wailing to beat the band, so I moseyed on over and asked her what the problem was.

"Ghosts!" she said, answering in heavily accented American.

"Ghosts?"

"In my attic," she said, crossing herself. "Every night I hear them, pacing the floors and rattling their chains. So I asked the church to send someone to exercise the ghost, and instead they sent that... that *buffoon*, who wouldn't know a ghost if it jumped up and spit on him."

"Well, I'm right sorry to hear it, ma'am."

"I even offered to pay a million lira to the church if they would just exercise my ghosts."

I couldn't figure out why she was so all fired anxious to have someone take her ghosts out for a walk, but suddenly I thought I saw a way to raise a little grubstake for me and my Silent Partner.

"Uh...how much is a million lira in real money, ma'am?" I said.

She didn't know, but she told me what it bought, and I figured we were talking close to a thousand dollars.

"Well, ma'am, I don't want to say nothing bad about our competitors, me being a decent Christian, but it appears to me that you've been dealing with the wrong church."

"What are you talking about?" she said.

"I'm the pastor of the Tabernacle of Saint Luke," I said, "and it just so happens that exercising ghosts is one of the very best things we do."

"Where is this Tabernacle?" she asked suspiciously.

"Well, truth to tell, it ain't quite built yet, but your kind donation could buy us the first cornerstone."

"I don't give money to any charlatan who comes around making promises," she said. "First you exercise my ghosts. *Then* I'll pay you."

"Ma'am, you got yourself a deal," I said with my very best Sunday go to meeting grin. "I'll exercise the tar out of the critters."

"They're never around in the daytime," she said. "Come back after dark."

"Sounds good to me, ma'am," I said. "I'll see you then."

I shook her hand, and went off to buy myself some lunch with the money I'd gotten from the tourists, and with what was left I stopped by a pet store and bought a couple of leashes so these here ghosts wouldn't try to get away from me while I was exercising 'em. Then I bought a flashlight, and a nice black bag to hold everything, and I spent the rest of the afternoon testing out half a dozen fine Italian wines, all of which had been aging at least since mid-morning, and finally the sun set and I went back to the lady's house and knocked on the door.

"I really didn't think you would come back," she said, and now that it was dark out her whole manner was different, like she was scared to death or something. If it had been me and I felt that way about ghosts, I'd have wanted 'em permanently removed from the premises instead of just given a workout, but there ain't no accounting for the peculiarities of the female mind, even though it's frequently attached to other parts that seem to make a lot more sense, so I just walked into the living room and asked her where the ghosts were at.

"Upstairs," she said with a shudder. "In the attic."

"Thanks a lot, ma'am," I said. "Just go about your business. I'll have 'em exercised in no time at all."

"What is that?" she asked, pointing to my black bag.

"It's got all my exercising equipment in it," I explained.

"You are the bravest man I have ever met," she said. "What is your name?"

"The Right Reverend Doctor Lucifer Jones at your service, ma'am," I said.

She stared at me for a good long time. "Are you married?" she said at last. "I have this beautiful young niece in Florence..."

"Well, actually, ma'am, I'm kind of married to the Lord, though He gets a mite fidgety when I refer to it that way." I looked around. "Which way to the attic? The sooner I get these here ghosts up and exercised, the sooner I can put your kind donation to use."

She pointed to a staircase. "Go up two flights, to the third floor," she said. "Then you will see a bolted wooden door leading up to the attic."

"Well, at least *I'm* gonna get exercised," I said, but she didn't understand my joke, leading me to conclude that middle-aged Italian widows ain't got no sense of humor, so I just smiled at her again and started climbing up the stairs. When I came to the wooden door on the third floor I slid back the bolt, opened it, and went up this narrow set of creaky stairs leading to the attic.

I pulled out the flashlight and turned it on. I hadn't never seen a ghost before, but I figured it'd be wearing a white sheet and floating a little bit off the floor, unless Italian ghosts were a lot different from American ones, but before I could look into every nook and cranny of the attic a huge unghostly hand reached out and grabbed me from behind.

"What are you doing here?" demanded a low voice.

"I ain't armed and I don't mean you no harm!" I said. "I'm just here to take you out for a little walk."

"Your voice sounds familiar," said whatever was holding me.

"Now as I come to think on it, so does yours," I said. "Let go of me so's I can get a look at you."

I twisted around and found myself facing this eight foot tall guy with brown hair and blue eyes. He hadn't shaved in a few weeks, but I didn't have no trouble recognizing him.

"Sam Hightower!" I exclaimed. "What in blazes are *you* doing here?"

"Lucifer Jones!" he said. "I was about to ask the same thing of you."

"I been commissioned to exercise such ghosts as may be setting up shop in this here attic," I said. "How about you? The last time I saw you, you'd given up the Abominable Snowman business and were hiding out from Guido Scarducci's friends and relations in Nepal."

"They found me," he said.

"He still ain't forgiven you for not shaving points in the big basketball game like you agreed to, huh?" I said.

"The man is totally without compassion," he answered. "I barely escaped with my life. They chased me all across Asia and into Europe, and I finally wound up in Rome."

"But why are you hiding out in an attic?"

"Well, it's mighty difficult to hide out in a crowd when you're eight feet two inches tall," he said. "I've been keeping to myself by day, and sneaking out to steal food at night."

"You know," I said, mulling on his situation, "I think I see a way for the two of us to make a profit out of your unhappy plight. Maybe even enough so that you can finally pay Guido Scarducci off and go back home without worrying about what might be gaining on you."

"Yeah?" he said. "What's your plan?"

"The old lady what owns this place is paying me a million lira to exercise you," I said, "but even a compassionate woman like her ain't likely to pay me to take you out for a walk each and every day. But," I added, "if you was to move down the block, or maybe around the corner, and do some serious moaning and wailing at night, I could probably get another million to turn you out into the street, and we can keep doing it as long as you can keep finding attics."

"It does have possibilities," he admitted thoughtfully. "And the best part of it is that no one would have to see me."

"Getting seen wouldn't exactly work to our advantage," I agreed.

"How will we manage it?" he asked.

"We'll just wait until the widder lady's gone to sleep, and sneak on down the stairs," I said, "and then you can point out the next house you plan to haunt. I'll stop by in the morning to collect my fee and explain that the ghosts ran off while I was exercising 'em and at least she ain't gonna be troubled by 'em no more. Then I'll give you a couple of evenings to stir up the owners of your next attic, after which I'll come by and offer my services again."

"Sounds good to me," he said. "We split all the fees fifty-fifty, right?"

"Wrong," I said. "One third for me, one third for you, and one third for the Lord."

He kept insisting that this was really a two-for-one split, so finally we struck a deal that he and I would split the first fifty million lira down the middle, and then the Lord had an option on the next ten million, at which point the three of us would renegotiate the contract.

Well, we sat around in the attic for a few hours, reminiscing about Tibet and Nepal, and he told me all about how he got chased through Russia by Guido Scarducci's gunmen, and I told him all about the Land of Eternal Youth and the Scorpion Lady and the home-made man and all the people and places I'd seen since we parted, and then it was close on to three o'clock and we could hear the widder lady snoring up a storm, so we gently and quietly descended the stairs and let ourselves out, and just before we parted company Sam Hightower pointed out the next attic he planned to haunt, and I took my last few dollars and rented a room for the night.

I came by in the morning and explained that the ghosts had all run off and hid once I got 'em outside, and before I could apologize or make excuses or nothing the lady had thrown her arms around me and kissed me and started thanking everyone from God to the Madonna to half a dozen local saints, although it was me and me alone what removed the ghosts, and then she paid me my million lira and kissed me again, and ran off to tell her neighbors the good news while I moseyed over to the Via Veneto and rented a suite at the Excelsior, which was the poshest hotel in Rome back in them days.

I figured to give Sam three nights to get the owners of his new domicile time to get used to the idea that they had more than mice in their attic, but the very next afternoon a little Italian feller with glasses and an umbrella came calling on me while I was grabbing some espresso at a local streetside cafe.

"You are Lucifer Jones, are you not?" he asked.

"The Right Reverend Lucifer Jones, at your service," I said, gesturing for him to join me, but he just stood there looking kind of nervous.

"Thank God I have found you!" he said. "Signora Mondedori described you to me, but nobody knew where you lived. I have been searching for you all day."

"Who's this Signora Mondedori?" I asked, wondering if I'd made any romantic promises that had slipped my mind in the past few hours.

"You removed the ghosts from her house."

"Oh, *that* Signora Mondedori," I said, much relieved.

"She lives across the street from us, and told us of your faith and your bravery," he said.

"Well, it comes from living a clean life and thinking nothing but pure thoughts," I said modestly. "And now that you've found me, what can I do for you, Signor...?"

"Signor Palusco," he said. "Enrico Palusco. I will come right to the point. I have lived in my house all my life. My father lived there for his entire life, as did my grandfather. Never have we had a cause to regret this. Never has there been any reason not to be content."

"I'm sure glad you're getting right to the point," I said.

"But last night," he continued, "I heard things in my attic!"

"What kind of things?" I asked.

"Unholy, supernatural things!" he said, his voice shaking. "Ghostly things! Horrible moaning and hideous screeching!"

"I'm right sorry to hear that, Brother Palusco," I said. "Sounds like your neighborhood has caught itself a plague of ghosts."

"Will you remove them from my house?" he asked.

"Well," I said, "I got a lot of exercising jobs lined up. To be truthful, I don't think I could get to your house much before next week. My best advice is to put all your affairs in order and scout out a reputable funeral parlor. These ghosts don't ordinarily devour a whole family at a single sitting, so there ought to be at least one survivor to see to the burials."

"I will pay you ten million lira if you come tonight!" he said. "I beg of you, Signor Jones!"

"Well, I really shouldn't sneak you in ahead of all these other needy families," I said, "but somehow you've touched my compassionate Christian heart. I'll be there with my exercising gear just after dark. Why don't you wait out front for me, to make sure I got the right address? I'd hate to wind up in the wrong house, since in my experience goblins and leprechauns don't take as well to exercising as ghosts do."

He kissed my hand and started muttering in Italian.

"And don't forget to have the money ready, Brother Palusco," I said as he began walking away.

Well, when I showed up, there must have been fifty people from the neighborhood all wanting to shake my hand and bless me and such, and I thanked 'em and told 'em to go back to their houses because exercising ghosts was a delicate and tricky business and could well take the whole night, and then I went up the stairs with my little black bag and found Sam wailing and moaning into a heating vent. I gave him a sandwich that I'd brung along, and then pulled a couple of beers out of my bag, and we sat around until we figured the rest of the world was asleep, and then we snuck on down the stairs and back into the street, and Sam chose his next attic, and the next day, even before I could come back for my money, Signor Palusco showed up at my hotel and paid me, and it was all I could do to get him to leave before he started kissing me so much that people began looking kind of strange at us, and one very clean-cut young man stopped by to tell me his name was Damon and he could usually be found hanging around the lobby in late afternoons.

Then a strange thing happened. Even though I knew Sam was only haunting one house at a time, word of my success at exercising spooks and spirits started making the rounds, and before evening I'd had another half a dozen requests from people that was sure they had ghosts in the attic, though after talking to 'em I figured what they mostly had was bats in the belfry.

Still, business looked so good that I figured I might as well rent out an office. I found myself a nice one over near the Spanish Steps, all furnished and everything, and even though the sign painter couldn't spell and wound up painting "Ghosts Exorcised" on the door, I was pretty well satisfied with the way things were going.

I exercised Hightower out of five more houses in the next two weeks, and we began thinking about expanding the business and maybe hiring a few more ghosts and a few more exercisers. We were still mulling it over when I escorted him out of yet another house in the middle of the night, and we decided that before we committed to taking on more help we ought to make sure that the market could bear it, so we decided to have him move his base of operations and start haunting a brand new neighborhood, just to see if we got the same reaction.

Well, we walked through the residential sections of Rome for maybe an hour, and finally, when we figured we'd put enough distance betwixt ourselves and our former stamping grounds, we turned onto the Via Aurelia. Hightower studied the area for a minute or two, then pointed to a house about halfway down the block and told me that was where he planned to set up shop. I couldn't see what it was about that particular house that attracted him when they all looked so much alike, but I figured that haunting was his business and unhaunting was mine, and I didn't want to make no intrusions in his area of professional expertise.

I spent the next day visiting my competition at the Vatican, mostly because I'd heard that they had a really fascinating collection of pornography, but evidently they didn't feel the need to share it with no outsiders, because I was told it was kept under lock and key and no one was allowed to see it, which struck me as just plumb wasteful, but even thought I put up a fuss and asked to see the head man they wound up escorting me out the door, and I returned to my office just in time to get a phone call from a Signor Crosetti who lived on the Via Aurelia and had just come down with a bad case of ghosts. I scribbled down his address and negotiated a fee, then promised him I'd be there an hour after sundown.

In the meantime, I had myself a nice dinner at the Sans Souci, where I'd took to reserving a regular table, and then picked up a couple of sandwiches and some beers to bring along for Hightower. Since it wasn't quite dark yet, I returned to the office to spend a few happy minutes counting our money and arranging it into artistic stacks and the like, and somehow or other I must have fallen asleep because the next thing I knew Signor Crosetti was on the phone, telling me that it was after midnight and his ghost was haunting up a storm.

When I showed up, Signor Crosetti was waiting for me out in front of his place with a lantern in his hand, all red of face and covered with sweat. He told me he'd sent his family off to spend the night with his brother, and he planned to join 'em just as soon as he let me into the house, and that nothing would ever get him to go inside again until I assured him that I'd whipped his ghost in straight falls and sent it packing.

This struck me as right considerate on his part, since it meant that Hightower and me could enjoy our beers in comfort in the living room before making our departure a few hours later, so I waited until he unlocked the front door and told him to show up at my office in the morning and I'd give him a blow by blow account of what went on.

Then I was inside the house, and the door slammed shut behind me, and I walked over to the staircase and pulled out my flashlight and shined the beam up to the next floor, where Hightower was moaning like there was no tomorrow.

"Hey, Hightower," I called out. "Come on down and have a beer. The coast is clear."

Nothing much happened except that he stopped moaning and started rattling a batch of chains that he must have found up there, or maybe swiped off someone's bicycle and brought along for the effect.

"Come on, Hightower!" I yelled. "This is me, Lucifer, calling to you. The house is empty!"

Hightower started making noises like unto a bull moose calling for his ladyfriend, and I started getting a little hot under the collar.

"Are you gonna make me climb all the way up there?" I said. "I keep telling you, there ain't no one else in the whole house except you and me!"

He got to moaning and wailing again, really sorrowful-like, and after a couple of minutes I gave up yelling at him and climbed up the stairs.

"Okay, Hightower," I said, shining the light around. "Where the hell are you hiding?"

He started moaning louder, and now I could tell he was up in the attic, and I figured that probably he just hadn't been able to hear me, and even though I was annoyed at having to climb all them stairs, I made up my mind to praise him for the way he was devoting himself to his work.

Problem was, when I finally reached the attic, there wasn't no one there. There was a heap of wailing, and I could hear some chains rattling in the corner, but I couldn't see hide nor hair of Hightower, and at eight feet two inches tall that was a lot of hide and hair to hide all at once.

"Come on now, Hightower," I said. "Fun's fun, but the beer's getting warm and I'm getting tired. Let's go on downstairs."

"*Go away!*" he whispered.

"What do you mean, go away?" I demanded. "Here I am being considerate enough to bring you some grub and some beer to wash it down with and you're getting temperamental?"

"*Leave me to my misery!*" he whispered.

"Your misery?" I said. "Look, I may have took a little more out of your half than mine for expenses, but that ain't no reason to—"

"*Go away!*" he whispered again.

"You tell me to go away once more and I just may do it!" I snapped. "I can always hire me another ghost, you know."

"Who are you talking to up there, Lucifer?" said a familiar voice. I looked back down the stairs and saw this eight-foot-tall figure climbing up to join me.

"Hightower?" I said.

"I was in the attic next door, and I saw you come into the wrong house," he said. "When you didn't come right back out, I figured I'd come over to see what was going on."

"You mean you're just getting here this second?" I said.

"That's what I just told you," he answered.

"And I suppose you ain't never studied to be a ventriloquist?"

"It ain't ever been one of my major ambitions," he said.

"Then I think we got a serious problem on our hands," I said.

"What are you talking about?"

"I'm all through talking," I said, heading down the stairs. "What I'm about to start doing now is beating a tactical retreat."

"What's so all-fired frightening about an attic?" he yelled after me.

"Attics don't scare me none," I hollered back. "It's what's *in* the attic that I don't want no part of!"

"I've been living in these old attics for months," he said, walking in. "I'll show you there's nothing to be afraid of."

"You do whatever you think's best," I said, as I reached the front door. "Me, I'm high-tailing it out of here."

I had just made it to the street when I heard a scream that would have woke such dead as weren't otherwise occupied, and a second later Hightower burst out of the house, yelling that he was heading for home and all Guido Scarducci and his friends and relations could do was kill him, and that wasn't nothing compared to what could happen to him in the attic. The last I saw of him he was running on a true course for Butte, Montana, and something about his manner implied that he wasn't gonna let a little thing like an ocean stand in his way.

As for me, I figured if I stayed in Rome people would keep asking me to get rid of their ghosts for them, and I had permanently retired from the exercising business the minute I ran out of Signor Crosetti's house, so I cleaned out the office, stuck all the money into my little black bag, and set out to find a suitable site to build my tabernacle.

6. THE WEREWOLF

After I left Italy I wandered north and west. A couple of months later I found myself in Hungary, which ain't never gonna provide the Riviera with any serious competition for tourists. Each town I passed through was duller than the last, until I got to Budapest, which was considerably less exciting than Boise, Idaho on a Tuesday afternoon.

I passed by an old, run-down arena that did double duty, hosting hockey games on weeknights and dog shows on Saturdays, then walked by the only nightclub in town, which was featuring one of the more popular lady tuba soloists in the country, and finally I came to the Magyar Hotel and rented me a room. After I'd left my gear there I set out to scout out the city and see if there were enough depraved sinners to warrant building my tabernacle there and setting up shop in the salvation business. My unerring instincts led me right to a batch of them, who were holed up in the men's room of the bus station, playing a game with which I was not entirely unfamiliar, as it consisted of fifty two pasteboards with numbers or pictures on 'em and enough money in the pot to make it interesting.

"Mind if I join you gents?" I asked, walking over to them.

"Either you put your shirt on backward, or else you're a preacher," said one of 'em in an English accent.

"What's that got to do with anything?" I asked.

"We'd feel guilty taking your money," he said.

"You ain't got a thing to worry about," I said, sitting down with them.

"Well," he said with a shrug, "you've been warned."

"I appreciate that, neighbor," I said, "and just to show my good will, I absolve everyone here of any sins they committed between nine o'clock this morning and noon. Now, who deals?"

The game got going hot and heavy, and I had just about broken even, when the British feller dealt a hand of draw, and I picked up my cards and fanned 'em out and suddenly I was looking at four aces and a king, and two of my opponents had great big grins on their faces, the kind of grin you get when you pick up a flush or a full house, and one of 'em opened, and the other raised, and I raised again, and it was like I'd insulted their manhood, because they raised right back, and pretty soon everyone else had dropped out and the three of us were tossing money into the pot like there wasn't no tomorrow, and just about the time we all ran out of money and energy and were about to show our cards, a little Hungarian kid ran into the room and shouted something in a foreign language—probably Hungarian, now as I come to think on it—and suddenly everyone grabbed their money and got up and started making for the exit.

"Hey, what's going on?" I demanded. "Where do you guys think you're going?"

"Away!" said the British feller.

"But we're in the middle of a hand," I protested.

"Lupo is coming!" said the Brit. "The game's over!"

"Who the hell is Lupo?" I demanded.

"He's more of a what. You'll leave too, if you know what's good for you!"

And suddenly, just like that, I was all alone in the men's room of a Hungarian bus station, holding four totally useless aces and a king, and thinking that maybe Hungarians were more in need of a shrink than a preacher. Then the door opened, and in walked this thin guy with grayish skin and hair everywhere—on his head, his lip, his chin, even the backs of his hands.

"Howdy, Brother," I said, and he nodded at me. "You better not plan on lingering too long," I added. "Someone or something called Lupo is on its way here."

He turned to face me and stared at me intently.

"I am Lupo," he said.

"You are?"

"Count Basil de Chenza Lupo," he continued. "Who are you?"

"The Right Reverend Doctor Lucifer Jones at your service," I said.

"Do you see any reason why you should run at the sight of me?" he continued.

"Except for the fact that you got a predatory look about you and probably ain't on speaking terms with your barber, nary a one," I answered.

"They are fools," he said. "Fools and peasants, nothing more."

"Maybe so," I said, "but you could have timed your call of Nature just a mite better, considering I was holding four bullets and the pot had reached a couple of thousand dollars."

"*Bullet?*" he said, kind of growling deep in his throat. "What kind?"

"Well, when you got four of 'em, there ain't a lot left except clubs, diamonds, hearts and spades," I said.

"But not silver?" he said.

"Not as I recollect."

"Good," he said, suddenly looking much relieved. "I am sorry I have caused you such distress, Doctor Jones."

"Well, I suppose when push comes to shove, it ain't really your fault, Brother Basil," I said.

"Nevertheless, I insist that you allow me to take you to dinner to make amends."

"That's right cordial of you," I said. "I'm a stranger in town. You got any particular place in mind?"

"We will dine at The Strangled Elk," he said. "It belongs to some Gypsy friends of mine."

"Whatever suits you," I said agreeably.

We walked out of the station, hit the main drag, and turned left.

"By the way, Brother Basil," I said, "why *were* all them men running away from a nice, friendly gent like you?"

He shrugged. "They are superstitious peasants," he said. "Let us speak no more of them."

"Suits me," I said. "People what entice a man of the cloth into a sinful game like poker and then run off when he's got the high hand ain't headed to no good end anyway."

I noticed as we walked down the street that everyone was giving us a pretty wide berth, and finally we turned down a little alleyway where all the men were dark and swarthy and wearing shirts that could have been took in some at the arms, and the women were sultry and good-looking and wearing colorful skirts and blouses, and Basil told me we were now among his Gypsy friends and no one would bother us, not that anyone had been bothering us before, and after a little while we came to a sign that said we'd reached The Strangled Elk, and we went inside.

It wasn't the cleanest place I'd ever seen, but I'd been a couple of weeks between baths myself, so I can't say that I minded it all that much. There was nobody there except one skinny old waiter, and Basil called him over and said something in Gypsy, and the waiter went away and came back a minute later with a bottle of wine and two glasses.

Well, we filled the glasses and chatted about this and that, and then we drank some more and talked some more, and finally the waiter brought out a couple of steaks.

"Brother Basil," I said, looking down at my plate, "I like my meat as rare as the next man, but I don't believe this has been cooked at all."

"I am sorry, my friend," he said. "That is the way I always eat it, and the cook simply assumed you shared my taste." He signaled to the waiter, said something else in Gypsy, and the waiter took my plate away. "It will be back in a few moments, properly cooked."

"You *always* eat your steak like that?" I asked, pointing to the slab of raw meat in front of him.

"It is the only way," he replied, picking it up with his hands and biting off a goodly chunk of it. He growled and snarled as he chewed it.

"You got a bit of a throat condition?" I asked.

"Something like that," he said. "I apologize if my table manners offend you."

"I've et with worse," I said. In fact, if push came to shove, I couldn't remember having dined with a lot that were much more refined.

Well, my steak came back just then, and after covering it with a pint of ketchup just to bring out the subtle nuances of its flavor, I dug in, and just so Basil wouldn't feel too conspicuous I growled and snarled too, and we spent the next five or ten minutes enjoying the noisiest meal of my experience, after which we polished off a couple of more bottles of wine.

"I have truly enjoyed this evening, my friend," said Basil after we were all done. "So few people will even speak to me, let alone join me in a repast…"

"I can't imagine why," I said. "You'd have to search far and wide to find a more hospitable feller."

"Nonetheless," he said, "it is time for you to leave."

"It's only about nine o'clock," I said. "I think I'll just sit here and digest the repast and maybe smoke a cigar or two, that is if you got any to spare, and then I'll mosey on back to my humble dwelling."

"You really must leave *now*," he said.

"You got a ladyfriend due any minute, right?" I said with a sly smile. "Well, never let it be said that Lucifer Jones ain't the soul of understanding and discretion. Why, I recall one time back in Cairo, or maybe it was Merrakech, that I…"

"*Hurry!*" he shouted. "The moon is rising!"

"Now how could you possibly know that, sitting here in the back of the room?" I asked.

"I *know!*" he said.

I got up and walked over to the doorway and stuck my head out. "Well, son of a gun, the moon *is* out," I said. "I don't see your ladyfriend nowhere, though."

I turned back to face him, but Count Basil de Chenza Lupo wasn't nowhere to be seen. In fact, there wasn't no one in the room except the old waiter and an enormous wolf that must have wandered in through the kitchen door.

"Well, I've heard of restaurants that got roaches," I said, "and restaurants that got rats, but I do believe this is the first eatery I ever been to that was infested by wolves." I turned to the waiter. "What happened to Basil?" I asked. "Did he go off to the necessary?"

The waiter shook his head.

"Then where is he?"

The waiter pointed to the wolf.

"I don't believe I'm making myself clear," I said. "I ain't interested in no four-legged critters with fleas and bad breath. Where is Basil?"

The waiter pointed to the wolf again.

"I don't know why it's so hard to understand," I said. "That there is a wolf. I want to know what became of Basil."

The waiter nodded his head. "Basil," he said, pointing at the wolf again.

"You mean the wolf is named Basil, too?" I asked.

The waiter just threw his hands up and walked out of the room, leaving me alone with the wolf.

Well, I looked at the wolf for a good long while, and he looked right back at me, and as time went by it occurred to me that I hadn't seen no other wolves in all my wanderings through Europe, and that some zoo ought to be happy to pay a healthy price for such a prime specimen, so I walked over kind of gingerly and let him smell the back of my hand, and when I was sure he wasn't viewing me as a potential appetizer, I slipped my belt out of my pants and slid it around his neck and turned it into a leash.

"You come along with me, Basil," I said. "Tonight you can sleep in my hotel room, and tomorrow we'll set about finding a properly generous and appreciative home for you."

I started off toward the door, but he dug his feet in and practically pulled my arm out of the socket.

"Now Basil," I said, jerking on the leash with both hands, "I ain't one to abuse dumb animals, but one way or the other you're coming with me."

He pulled back and whimpered, and then he snarled, and then he just went limp and laid down, but I was determined to get him out of there, and I started dragging him along the floor, and finally he whined one last time and got to his feet and started trotting alongside of me, and fifteen minutes later we reached the door of the Magyar Hotel. I had a feeling they had some policy or other regarding wild critters in the rooms, so I waited until the desk clerk went off to flirt with one of the maids, and then I opened the door and me and Basil made a beeline for the staircase, and reached the second floor without being seen. I walked on down the corridor until I came to my room, unlocked it, and shagged Basil into it. He looked more nervous and bewildered than vicious, and finally he hopped onto the couch and curled up and went to sleep, and I lay back down on the bed and drifted off while I was trying to figure out how many thousands of dollars a real live wolf was worth.

Except that when I woke up, all set to take Basil the wolf off to the zoo, he wasn't there. Instead, laying naked on the couch and snoring up a storm, was Basil the Count, with my belt still around his neck.

I shook him awake, and he sat up, startled, and began blinking his eyes.

"You got something highly personal and just a tad improbable that you want to confide in me, Brother Basil?" I said.

"I *tried* to warn you," he said plaintively. "I told you to leave, to hurry."

"You considered seeing a doctor about this here condition?" I said. "Or maybe a veterinarian?"

He shook his head miserably. "It is a Gypsy curse," he said at last. "There is nothing that can be done about it. I am a werewolf, and that's all there is to it."

"And that's why all them guys were running away from you at the station and looking askance at you on the street?"

He nodded. "I am an outcast, a pariah among my own people."

"Yeah, well, I can see how it probably hampers your social life," I opined.

"It has hampered *all* aspects of my life," he said unhappily. "I have seen so many charlatans and *poseurs* trying to get the curse removed that I am practically destitute. I cannot form a lasting relationship. I dare not be among strangers when the moon comes out. And some of the behavior carries over: you saw me at the dinner table last night."

"Well, it may have been a bit out of the ordinary," I said soothingly, "but as long as you don't lift you leg on the furniture, I don't suppose anyone's gonna object too strenuously. Especially since if they object at the wrong time of day, there's a strong possibility they could wind up getting et."

"You are the most understanding and compassionate man I've ever met, Doctor Jones," he said, "but I am at the end of my tether. I don't know what to do. I have no one to turn to. Only these accursed Gypsies will tolerate my presence, because it amuses them. I think very soon I shall end it all."

At which point the Lord smote me with another of His heavenly revelations.

"Seems to me you're being a mite hasty, Brother Basil," I said.

"What is the use of going on?" he said plaintively. "I will never be able to remove the curse."

"First of all, you got to stop thinking of your condition as a curse," I continued. "What if I was to show you how the werewolf business could be a blessing in disguise?"

"Impossible!"

"You willing to bet five thousand dollars on that?" I asked.

"What are you talking about?" he demanded.

"You see," I said, "the problem is that you ain't never really examined yourself when the moon is out. You ain't simply a werewolf, but you happen to be a damned fine-looking werewolf."

"So what?"

"On my way into town, I passed an arena that holds a dog show every Saturday. The sign said that the prize money was ten thousand dollars."

"You just said five," he pointed out.

"Well, me and the Lord have got to have a little something to live on, too," I said.

"What makes you think a wolf can win a dog show?" he said dubiously.

"Why don't you just concentrate on being a handsome, manly type of critter and let *me* worry about the rest of it?" I said.

Well, we argued it back and forth for the better part of the morning, but finally he admitted that he didn't see no better alternatives, and he could always commit suicide the next week if things didn't work out, and I went off to buy a leash and some grooming equipment at the local pet store, and then stopped by the arena for an entry form. I didn't know if he had an official werewolf name or not, so I just writ down Grand International Champion Basil on the form, and let it go at that.

The biggest problem I had the next two days was finding a vet who was open at night, so I could get Basil his rabies and distemper shots, but finally I convinced one to work late for an extra fifty dollars, which I planned to deduct from Basil's share of the winnings, since the shots didn't do me no good personally, and then it was Saturday, and we just stuck around the hotel until maybe five in the afternoon, Basil getting more and more nervous, and finally we walked on over to the arena.

Basil's class was scheduled to be judged at seven o'clock, but as the hour approached it began to look like the moon wasn't going to come out in time, and since I didn't want us to forfeit all that money by not showing up on time, I quick ran out into the alley, grabbed the first couple of cats I could find, and set 'em loose in the arena. The newspaper the next morning said that the ruckus was so loud they could hear it all the way over in Szentendre, which was a little town about forty miles up the road, and by the time everything had gone back to normal Basil was about as far from normal as Hungarian counts are prone to get, and I slipped his leash on him and headed for the ring.

There were three other dogs ahead of us, and after we entered the ring the judge came over and look at Basil.

"This is a class for miniature poodles," he said severely. "Just what kind of mongrel is *that*?"

"You know this guy, Basil?" I asked.

Basil nodded.

"He one of the ones who's mean to you when you walk through town?"

Basil growled an ugly growl.

"*Basil?*" said the judge, turning white as a sheet.

Basil gave him a toothy grin.

"Now, to answer your question," I said, "this here happens to be a fully growed miniature poodle what takes umbrage when you insults its ancestry."

The judge stared at Basil for another couple of seconds, then disqualified the other three dogs for not looking like him and handed me a blue ribbon.

Well, to make a long story short, old Basil terrorized the judges in the next three classes he was in and won 'em all, and then the ring steward told me that I had five minutes to prepare for the final class of the day, where they would pick the best dog in the show and award the winner the ten thousand dollars.

Suddenly Basil started whining up a storm. I couldn't see no ticks or fleas on him, and he couldn't tell me what was bothering him, but something sure was, and finally I noticed that he was staring intently at something, and I turned to see what it was, and it turned out to be this lovely-looking lady who was preparing to judge the Best in Show class.

"What's the problem, Basil?" I asked.

He kept whining and staring.

"Is it *her*?"

He nodded.

I racked my mind trying to figure out what it was about her that could upset him so much.

"She's been mean to you before?" I asked.

He shook his head.

"She's got something to do with the Gypsies who cursed you?"

He shook his head again.

"I can't figure out what the problem is," I said. "But what the hell, as long as we let her know who you are, it's in the bag."

He pointed his nose at the ceiling and howled mournfully.

"She's from out of town and doesn't know you're a werewolf?" I asked with a sinking feeling in the pit of my stomach.

He whimpered and curled up in a little ball.

"Will the following dogs please enter the ring?" said the announcer. "Champion Blue Boy, Champion Flaming Spear, Champion Gladiator, Champion Jericho, and Grand International Champion Basil."

Well, we didn't have no choice but to follow these four fluffy little dogs into the ring. The judge just stared at us for a minute with her jaw hanging open, and I figured we were about to get booted out, but then she walked over and knelt down and held Basil by the ears and peered into his face, and then she stood up and stepped back a bit and stared at him some more, and finally she walked over to me and said, "This is the most handsome, rugged, masculine dog I have ever seen. I have a female I'd love to breed to him. Is he for sale?"

I told her that I was just showing him for a friend, and that she'd have to speak to the Count de Chenza Lupo about it later. She scribbled down her address, and it turned out that she was staying three rooms down the hall from me at the Hotel Magyar.

Finally she examined the other four dogs briefly and with obvious disinterest, and then she announced that Grand International Champion Basil was the best dog in this or any other show and had won the ten thousand dollars.

Well, Basil and me stuck around long enough to have a bunch of photos taken for the papers and then high-tailed it back to the hotel, where we waited until daylight and he became Count Basil again and we divvied up the money. Then he walked down the hall to talk to the judge about selling himself to her, and he came back half an hour later with the silliest grin on his face and announced that he was in love and she didn't mind in the least that he was a werewolf and all was right with the world.

I read in the paper that the other dog owners were so outraged about losing to a wolf that they tore the building down, and with the dog shows canceled for the foreseeable future I couldn't see no reason to stick around, so I bid Hungary farewell and decided to try my luck in Paris, where I'd heard tell that the sinners were so thick on the ground you could barely turn around without making the real close acquaintanceship of at least a couple of 'em.

I never saw old Basil again, but a few months later I got a letter from him. He'd married his lady judge and left Budapest for good, and was living on her country estate managing her kennel—and he added a proud little postscript that both his wife and her prize female were expecting.

7. THE CLUBFOOT OF NOTRE DAME

If you wander down the Champs Élysées today, or mosey over to Montmartre or the Trocadero or the Latin Quarter, you can still find a few people who remember me, even though I haven't been there since 1933.

Therefore, I think it's only fair that I tell you *my* side of the story.

I hit Paris in late afternoon of a lovely spring day in April, and even before I had time to line up a hotel and hunt up a place to eat, I found myself in a mild disagreement with some of the locals concerning exactly how many aces there were supposed to be in the deck I was dealing from, and just as things were starting to get ugly, the local constabularies rescued me and thoughtfully lined up my room and board for the next week, all at public expense.

Now, while I wouldn't never want to complain about such generous treatment, I'd be less than my usual forthright and honest self if I didn't point out that the prison fare in Paris don't quite measure up to quality of grub you get at Maxim's or the Tour d'Argent, and the beds weren't quite as luxurious as you might expect at the Plaza Athénée or the Ritz. But given the price, I didn't have no real serious objections, and I was almost sorry to leave when they gave me my walking papers a week later.

I stopped at a sidewalk cafe, which didn't cater to no locals but was filled to overflowing with bearded American writers, all of 'em with tortured artistic eyes, and after I'd et some snails and washed them down with a bottle of wine, I realized that I still didn't have no place to stay.

I couldn't see no sense wasting any money on one of the more expensive hotels, so I started wandering around, kind of testing the waters to see if I could rent a room and a companion of the female persuasion for the price of a room alone, and pretty soon I found myself in an alley, and I came to this big door, and I could hear all kinds of laughing and clapping on the other side of it, like folks were having a real good time, so I opened it and stepped inside.

It was dark, and there were all kinds of theatrical-type props lying around, and about twenty yards off I could see a light, so I went in its direction, and suddenly I found myself face to face with this beautiful blonde lady who had evidently dressed in kind of a hurry, because she wasn't wearing nothing but a pair of high heels and a bunch of feathers in her hair.

"Howdy, ma'am," I said. "I heard the sound of merrymaking out in the alley, and I just followed my ears."

She looked kind of startled, and shot me a quick grin, and whispered, "Who are you?"

"The Right Reverend Doctor Lucifer Jones at your service, ma'am," I said. "If you ain't got no serious plans for the rest of the evening, I'd be happy to escort you to some of the finer night spots in town."

Suddenly I heard a roar of laughter off to my left, and I turned and saw a bunch of people sitting at tables, all of 'em laughing their heads off.

"Am I intruding in some kind of private party, ma'am?" I asked.

"You are intruding on the stage of the Follies Bergère, you fool!" she snapped.

"Does that mean you *ain't* available for an evening of fun and frolic?" I asked.

"Don't you understand?" she hissed. "You're interrupting a performance!"

"Where I come from, ladies don't perform wearing nothing but a smile," I said. Then I mulled on it a bit, and added, "Maybe that's why I left, now that I come to think on it."

The audience laughed again, and then I was surrounded by maybe two dozen more ladies who weren't wearing no more than the first, and it seemed that as long as I was there, and a stranger in town, the least I could do was introduce myself to each of 'em. I'd gotten about halfway down the line when they all started dancing across the stage, and I was left standing there all alone, so I figured

I might as well dance after 'em. Now, the waltz is just about the only dance I know, and it's right difficult to do without a partner, but I done the best I could, and just as I caught up with them a bunch of gendarmes started walking toward the stage, and even though I knew I was innocent of all wrongdoing, I didn't like the look in their eyes, so once I got near the curtain I just kept on waltzing, but the second I was offstage the audience started screaming something in French, and a minute later the stage manager ran up to me.

"They want more of you!" he said breathlessly.

"Well, of course they do," I said. "With all the old guys who stare at 'em night after night, it's probably been years since they was approached by a good-looking young buck like myself."

"I don't mean the girls," he said. "I mean the audience!"

"I don't think I follow you, Brother," I said.

"They think you're a clown, that you're part of the act. They want an encore!"

"An encore?" I repeated.

"What else can you do?"

"I'm a preacher by trade," I said. "I suppose if push came to shove I could give 'em a rouser about the Song of Solomon."

"Just get out there and do *something*!" said the stage manager, shoving me out into the spotlights.

The audience stopped yelling then, and settled back into their chairs.

"Howdy, folks," I said. "I'm the Right Reverend Lucifer Jones, and I've come to bring the word of the Lord into your dull, lackluster lives."

Well, for some reason or other, that brought forth a burst of chuckles, and I figured as long as they seemed to be in a partying mood, I'd warm 'em up with the story about the peg-legged whaler and the fireman's daughter before I got down to serious business, and they liked that one so much I followed it up with the one about the schoolmarm and the left-handed plumber, and by this time even the gendarmes were having a good time, and I figured I might as well put off any serious sermonizing til Sunday morning rolled around, and I told 'em a couple of more tales I'd accumulated during my travels to distant and exotic lands, and even though they didn't understand the one about the bow-legged jade merchant and the mandarin's daughter they laughed anyway, and we were having a high old time when the manager slipped me a note saying the girls were in serious danger of catching cold if they didn't start generating a little body heat, and I writ back that I may well have had the strength of ten because my heart was pure but I had counted twenty-five of 'em and he'd have to send fifteen of 'em home, and he wrote back to say I'd misunderstood him and what he meant was that he wanted me to get off the stage so they could go back to dancing.

Well, I didn't want none of them frail flowers coming down with a cold because of me, so I thanked the audience for being so friendly to a foreigner, and told them to stop by my tabernacle if they ever felt in serious need of salvation.

"Where is it?" asked one old geezer.

"I ain't had time to set up shop yet," I said. "But if any of you gents or ladies can suggest a good location, I'm willing to listen."

"Notre Dame!" said another, and everyone guffawed, and then I left the stage and the girls started working up a sweat, and the manager walked over to me.

"I don't know whether I should arrest you for interrupting the show, or offer you a long-term contract," he said. "I think I shall settle for politely showing you the door."

"Well, you *could* do me one favor, Brother," I said.

"And what is that?"

"Tell me about this Notre Dame," I said. "I always knew they played football. I didn't know they saved souls, too."

"It is the greatest church in the world," he said, looking at me like I had some kind of rare tropical disease. "How can you not know of it?"

"I know of it," I said with some dignity. "But I was under the impression that it was somewhere in Indiana."

He shook his head. "It is at the Ile de la Cite." I asked him to tell me how to get there, since I figured if I could get in tight with Knute Rockne or whoever was coaching the team these days I might get a little inside information that would help me beat the point spread, and then I thanked him for his help, bade him a fond farewell, and started walking down the lonely, deserted streets of Paris.

It must have been close to four in the morning when I got there, and let me tell you, it was one mighty impressive sight, even if I couldn't spot the stadium in the dark. There were gargoyles galore, one in particular bringing back memories of Honor Weinberger, a girl I'd known back in Moline, Illinois, and all kinds of stained glass windows, including a big rose-colored one, and finally I opened the door and walked inside. Someone was playing some mighty mournful music on the pipe organ, but I couldn't see who it was. In fact, it was so dark in there that I couldn't even see the ceiling, and after I'd looked around a bit and drunk in the architecture, of which there was an awful lot to drink in, I decided to see if I could hunt up the locker room, so I opened a door and started moseying down this corridor, which led to a batch of other corridors and doors, and pretty soon I couldn't hear the music no more and I was pretty well nigh lost, so I figured I'd retrace my steps and wait until daylight and maybe hunt up Knute and the gang at their practice field, but as I turned I saw this ugly little feller kind of shuffling after me. He looked like he knew his way around a lot better than I did, so I walked over to him on the assumption that he might be able to help me.

"Good evening, Brother," I said. "Was that you playing on the organ?"

He nodded. "I do it to relax, when nobody's around."

"You're right good at it."

He smiled a homely kind of smile. "Thank you very much." He paused. "Who are you, by the way?"

"I'm the Right Reverend Lucifer Jones, and I'm looking for the team's headquarters."

"Team?" he repeated. "What team?"

"The varsity, of course," I said. "Can't make no money betting on freshman games."

"We don't have any teams here," he said. "This is Notre Dame."

"I'm afraid that you been misinformed," I told him. "It just so happens that you got a top-notch football team."

He smiled. "That is the Notre Dame in America."

"You mean there's more than one of you?" I said.

He nodded.

"You know," I said, "I been thinking all night that it seemed like you guys scheduled an awful lot of road games. I guess that explains it."

"Well, now that you're here, why don't you join me in a glass of wine?" he said.

"That's mighty neighborly of you," I replied.

"It gets lonely here at night," he explained. "You're the first person I've seen in weeks."

"Well, you must see 'em when you go home in the mornings."

"I live here," he said. "My room is over by the belltower. I haven't set foot outside the church in, oh, it must be close to thirty years now."

We reached this little room that had a table and four chairs, and while I sat down, he limped over to a cabinet and pulled out two glasses and a bottle of red wine.

"Looks like you twisted your ankle," I said.

"It is a permanent condition," he said. "I'm a clubfoot."

"Well, I don't suppose it makes much difference, as long as no one's kicking field goals around here."

"I *like* you, Reverend Jones," he said, filling the glasses. "You are a very understanding man."

"And you are a very generous host," I said. "I want to thank you for the wine, Brother...?"

"Quesadilla."

"Brother Quesadilla," I concluded.

"You didn't laugh," he noted.

"Did someone tell a joke?"

"No," he said. "But my name...the Spanish seem to find it amusing."

"Well, the Spanish are easily amused," I said. "Usually a dead bull will do the trick."

"I like you more and more," he said. "No one has ever conversed so freely with me."

"Why not?" I said. "You seem like a friendly enough feller."

"Who knows? They hear the rumors, and..." He spread his hands and shrugged.

"Uh...just what kind of rumors are you referring to, Brother Quesadilla?" I asked.

"Oh, that I kidnap women and do grotesque things to them in the belltower," he said with a shrug.

"Sounds noisy," I allowed.

"On my honor, Reverend Jones, I have never taken a single woman to the belltower."

My first impulse was to ask if he took married women there. My second impulse was to ask if he didn't take 'em to the belltower, where *did* he take 'em? Then I took a serious look at all the muscles on his arms and neck, and my third and most reasonable impulse was to change the subject, which I proceeded to do.

"Brother Quesadilla," I said, "I been looking for a place to establish my tabernacle. As long as Fate has brung me to your doorstep, how much do you think your employers would rent this joint out for?"

He chuckled at that. "This is the Notre Dame Cathedral. It's not for rent, Reverend Jones."

"Well, here it is, four in the morning, and not a soul is milling around except you and me," I pointed out. "It seems a sorry waste of such a nice tasteful building."

"You preach to your congregation at four in the morning?" he asked.

"Well, truth to tell, I had in mind something more in the way of maybe a nightly bingo tournament to help pay the overhead."

"Bingo?" he said, puzzled.

"Well, if the French don't play bingo, I suppose we could set up a craps table and maybe a roulette wheel."

"It's a fascinating concept," he admitted with a grin, "but this is a place of worship."

"Brother Quesadilla, you'd be surprised how often people call upon the Good Lord when they got a pair of dice in their hands," I said.

He considered it for a minute and then shook his head sadly. "They'd never permit it."

"Wouldn't nobody have to know about it except you and me and such various sinners as we manage to attract," I said. "We could set up shop every night from, say, midnight til five in the morning."

"We?" he repeated.

"As in you and me," I said.

"Do you mean you'd really trust the notorious Clubfoot of Notre Dame?"

"Sure," I said. "I just won't go to the belltower with you."

"This is a most intriguing concept," he said. "Would we split the profits down the middle?"

"One third for you, one third for me, and one third for the Lord," I said.

"As the Lord's landlord, I'll hold His share of the money," said Quesadilla.

"I was kind of figuring on holding it myself," I replied, "me being His spokesman and all."

"Fifty-fifty?" he said.

I sighed. "Fifty-fifty," I agreed.

"How do you plan to get word to all the sinners?" he asked.

"I met a batch of 'em tonight," I said. "I'll just go on back to the same place tomorrow and announce that we're open for preaching, salvation, and craps."

"We'll need some craps tables and a roulette wheel," noted Quesadilla.

"Well, I figure if I'm supplying the sinners, the very least the landlord can do is supply the equipment."

He mulled on it for a minute or two and then agreed.

We shook hands, and I left him playing on the pipe organ. Then I hunted up a nearby hotel, which had seen better days and probably better centuries. I figured I was moving up to more elegant quarters the next night, but I didn't see no need to insult the management, so I registered for a week and the next morning I tiptoed out while the desk clerk was otherwise occupied.

There wasn't much for me to do until after dinnertime, so I decided to mosey on over to the Louvre and soak up a little culture. I saw everyone clustered around this one painting, and I figured it must be something pretty special, so I stood in line until I could get a good close look at it, but it turned out to be a picture of this kind of plain woman who couldn't quite make up her mind whether to smile at the painter or not, and in truth it didn't hold a candle to the picture of Nellie Willoughby in the altogether that they had hanging over the Long Bar of the New Stanley Hotel back in Nairobi.

I wandered around a bit more, and then I came to this statue of a lady who wasn't wearing an awful lot more that the ladies I'd seen the previous night, and it set my good artistic blood to boiling, because someone had busted off the arms out of sheer malicious mischief, and since it hadn't been covered up or repaired or nothing I figured the guards didn't know about it yet, so I hunted up a gendarme and grabbed him by the arm and led him over to the statue and pointed out what had happened and told him he'd better report it to his superior and maybe double their security until the culprit was caught. He just looked at me like I posed a serious danger, and right on the instant I realized that it was an inside job, and he didn't want to let his superiors know that he'd had any part of it, so I apologized for taking his time, and made a mental note to come back on his day off, and lay out the whole plot to whoever was in charge of the place after first finding out if there was a reward for exposing the culprits.

After I left the Louvre, I found I still had some time on my hands, so I wandered over to the Arc de Triomphe, which I'd always thought was a horse race but turned out to be a kind of big stone arch as well, though for the life of me I couldn't see how you could bet on it. I saw a bunch of Frenchmen standing around not doing much of anything, so I walked over and told 'em that they looked like a sporting lot, and that they could now do their sinning and their repenting all in the same spot if they'd come to Notre Dame a bit after midnight. Most of 'em thought I was kidding, but three or four guys writ down the information, and I told 'em to make sure they passed the word to all their friends and relations.

I stopped at a sidewalk cafe for dinner, and got a little live entertainment with my meal when a couple of bearded Americans wearing turtlenecks and berets got into a knock-down-drag-out over which of 'em looked more like Hemingway. In point of fact, the only Hemingway I knew was bald and eighty and ran a hardware store back in Ephrata, Pennsylvania, but I didn't see no sense hurting their feelings by enlightening 'em, and before long the gendarmes came along and dragged 'em both off to the hoosegow just as I was finishing my dessert.

By then it was time to go back to the Follies Bergère. I figured I'd just hunt up M. Bergère and ask him to make the announcement for me, but nobody in the whole place had seen hide nor hair of him, so I waited until the place filled up and then hopped onto the stage. Evidently I interrupted the very same blonde lady I had interrupted the night before, because she bellowed *"You again!"* and took off a shoe and started hammering me with it.

The audience thought it was all part of the show, and I recognized some of the same faces from the last time, so after I calmed the young lady down I told 'em a couple of more stories, including the one about the airplane pilot and the Tasmanian belly dancer, and then, when they'd all stopped laughing, I explained to them that Notre Dame had a new policy of one-stop sinning and salvation, and even though most of 'em laughed at first I kept explaining it over and over until everybody got right serious and the stage manager kept making a gesture with his hand across his throat, which I figured meant he was choking on a peach pit or something, and finally I thanked 'em for their time and hospitality and promised to greet any and all of 'em that came to Notre Dame later in the evening, and before I left the building I'd hired half a dozen refined young naked ladies to provide a little entertainment for our parishioners between midnight and sunrise.

I was thinking of stopping by the Lido and the Moulin Rouge and making the same announcement, but I noticed it was getting on toward ten o'clock and I decided I'd better get back to Notre Dame and see how Quesadilla was coming along with his part of the bargain.

Well, somehow or other, he'd managed to find a couple of roulette tables and three craps tables, and had even hunted up some poker and baccarat tables as well. I asked him if he knew anyone in the beer and wine business, so we could get a little liquid refreshment into them sinners what was running low on energy, and he said that he'd already thought of that, and couldn't see no reason to pay a middleman to set up a bar when we could do it ourselves, and just as he was explaining it to me in came a couple of deliverymen with our supplies.

We broke out a bottle of our best drinking stuff to celebrate our little enterprise, and then we settled back to wait for the sinners to start gathering, and sure enough, just after midnight, in they came, and by three in the morning we must have had a good four hundred evil men and painted women gambling their money away. Then at five o'clock we closed all the tables, and I stood up on a chair and forgave 'em in the name of my merciful and compassionate Silent Partner, and then they all went home, and me and Quesadilla paid off the young ladies and moved all the tables and supplies into a storeroom and counted up our take.

"Sixteen thousand francs!" he said excitedly.

"There's a lot to be said for working on the side of the Lord," I agreed.

"I never realized how well salvation could pay," he said.

"Well, it's all a matter of getting the right class of people in your congregation," I said. "Them what's beyond redemption usually ain't got all that much pocket money, and them what's totally without sin are probably more likely to throw the first stone than place the first bet."

Well, I found to my surprise that he liked talking religion as much as I did, so we kept it up til after sunrise, and then a batch of priests showed up and Quesadilla decided to head off to bed, and I watched the poorbox for a while and decided that the priests were missing a bet and that maybe once I got to know 'em better I'd explain to 'em how to run their church more like a business, but for the time being I decided they probably didn't want no outsiders interfering with the way they practiced their trade, so I headed toward the exit, and just as I did I bumped into a big roly-poly guy in priest's robes.

"Excuse me, Brother," I said. "I hope I didn't do you no lasting harm."

"I'm fine, my son," he replied. "Didn't I see you here very early yesterday morning as well?"

"It's a possibility," I said. "I hang around churches a lot, me being a man of the cloth and all."

"Episcopalian?" he asked.

"That's right generous of you," I answered, "but it's a little early in the day for me."

He just stared at me for a minute. "Well, if you should ever need help, I'm Father Gaston."

"I'll keep it in mind," I promised him. "And if you ever feel the need of spiritual uplifting, I'm the Right Reverend Honorable Doctor Lucifer Jones."

Well, he kept on staring at me for so long that I figured he was a little bit near-sighted and had maybe forgot his glasses, so finally I just smiled at him and continued on out the door, after which I decided that I needed someplace a little more upscale to hang my hat, so I hopped a taxicab and pulled up at the Ritz a few minutes later. I found out at the desk that they didn't give no discounts to clergymen, but I figured that as long as I was already there I might as well rent myself a room, and I spent the rest of the morning and afternoon doing a little serious sleeping.

Business was booming that night, as word of our little enterprise seemed to have spread far and wide, and it kept getting better all through the week. Every morning I would leave just after sunrise, and bump into Father Gaston, and exchange a few pleasantries with him, and every evening I would round up the ladies from the Follies Bergère and cart 'em over to Notre Dame and make sure that Quesadilla didn't invite none of 'em up to the belltower for a little hanky panky, and I was just about sure I'd finally found my calling, and was even thinking about scaring up some other churches and maybe franchising the salvation business, when one night, just when the young ladies were doing their artistic interpretation of an Indian love dance to Quesadilla's accompaniment on the pipe organ, and the mayor himself had two thousand francs riding on the next roll of the dice, Father Gaston burst into the church.

"What is going on here?" he demanded, and suddenly all our parishioners dropped what they were doing and high-tailed it for the exits, except for the young ladies, who weren't exactly dressed for going outside in the cool evening breeze.

"Well, howdy, Father Gaston," I said. "What brings you here at this ungodly hour?"

"Ungodly is the word for it!" he bellowed. "I had a feeling all week that something strange was going on here. What are you doing in my church?"

"Acquiring a first-rate congregation of sinful men and loose women," I explained. "After all, if they didn't have nothing to confess, you wouldn't need them little booths, would you?"

"This is outrageous!" he said. "Look at those women!"

"I can hardly take my eyes off 'em," I agreed admiringly. "Especially the third from the left."

"They're all naked!"

"Not much gets past your watchful eye, does it?" I said, figuring a little compliment, one clergyman to another, might help to calm him down.

"Why are they here?"

"Where else are a passel of naked ladies gonna go to find forgiveness?" I said. "I'd say Notre Dame has outdone itself tonight."

"And what were all those other people doing here?" he continued.

"Getting all the sin and corruption out of their systems so they'd be fit for saving," I said.

He stared at the tables. "Do you mean to tell me there's been gambling going on here?"

"No, I sure didn't mean to tell you that," I answered.

"I didn't mean to tell him anything," Quesadilla said unhappily.

"I'm calling the gendarmes this instant!" said Father Gaston.

"It won't do no good," I pointed out. "All our dealers and croupiers are gone. Tell 'em to come by tomorrow about midnight, and to bring plenty of money with 'em."

"You are impossible!" he shouted at me, and then turned to Quesadilla. "I hold you responsible for this, you ugly little clubfoot!"

"I don't care," said Quesadilla. "Reverend Jones is my friend. In fact, he's my *only* friend, and I won't let you do anything bad to him."

"He's a criminal and a fraud!" growled Father Gaston.

"Why don't you come up to the belltower with me and we'll discuss it?" suggested Quesadilla with a funny kind of smile on his face.

"We have nothing to discuss," said Father Gaston. "I'm having you both arrested."

"I don't think that would be a very good idea," said Quesadilla.

"Nobody asked you your opinion," said Father Gaston.

"If I go to court, they might ask me more than my *opinion*," said Quesadilla. "They might even ask me what I saw you doing with Madame Duchard."

"That was seventeen years ago!" said Father Gaston uneasily.

"Oh, I'll just tell them what I saw," said Quesadilla. "You can fill in the dates and other particulars."

"All right," said Father Gaston with a defeated sigh. "No gendarmes. Just get out of here and don't come back."

"That suits me fine," said Quesadilla. "Thirty years of this place is enough for me."

"Hah!" said Father Gaston. "Where is an ugly little clubfoot like you going to find work? You'll starve within a month."

"Father Gaston," I said, "as one man of the cloth to another, I'm ashamed to hear you carrying on like this to a decent Christian like Quesadilla who never meant no one any harm, and we ain't going to listen to no more of it."

I took Quesadilla by the arm and led him out the door, while Father Gaston just stood and glared at us.

"He's right, you know," said Quesadilla, as we walked down the empty Paris streets. "I've been cooped up there for thirty years. How am I ever going to make a living? I don't have any job skills."

"Sure you do," I said. "And with a little help from me, you ain't gonna have no trouble atall."

"What did you have in mind?" he asked curiously.

"Did you ever hear the one about the bullfighter and the fan dancer?" I asked.

"No, but—"

"Then shut up and listen."

Well, I told it to him, and as depressed as he was, he practically fell down laughing, so I told him to get himself a pen and paper, and once he did I sat down and told him the one about the poet and the feather merchant's twin daughters, and then the one about the Sumo wrestler and the circus thin lady, and the one about the six-fingered gangster and the one-eyed manicurist, and by the time the sun had come up I've guv him about a hundred such knee-slappers.

Then, after we had breakfast, I took him over to the Follies Bergère and introduced him to the stage manager, and after he told a couple of jokes they hit it right off, and the last I saw of the Clubfoot of Notre Dame, he was providing the musical accompaniment for the dancing girls at the organ and telling the audience droll stories between acts.

As for me, I took my half of the money and headed off to London, where I hoped to find a church that was more attuned to my particular brand of salvation.

8. THE CROWN JEWELS

The very first thing you notice about London is that it ain't exactly warm. The second thing is that it ain't exactly cold. The third is that it ain't exactly dry. The fourth is that it ain't exactly sunny. The fifth is that it ain't exactly cheap.

Still, London's got a lot of things going for it. For one thing, most of the folks speak a kind of American, which was a pleasant change from Paris, where they don't speak no known language at all. For another, everyone kept saying that it was a pretty class-ridden town, so I figured if I could just find out where the sinful classes hung out I'd know right where to establish my tabernacle.

I took a room at an old, run-down hotel on Basil Street, then went out looking for a sinner or two of the female persuasion, just to test the waters, so to speak. I'd got maybe three blocks away from the hotel when I came across a large crowd lined up to get into some theater, and they seemed so eager and excited that I decided I might as well join 'em and see what all the fuss was about, since in my broad experience on four continents very few entertainments draw that kind of enthusiasm unless they feature a few fallen women in serious need of both clothing and redemption.

Well, we all filed in and sat down, and while I was looking for painted women, of which there was nary a sign, an announcer came out on the bare stage and said, "Thank you for coming, ladies and gentlemen. Our speaker tonight needs no introduction. He has consented to give one of his rare public lectures, and so may I present, without any further *adieu*, the greatest consulting detective in the world, London's own Sherringford House."

Everybody stood up and started clapping, and then this skinny guy, dressed in tweeds and smoking a pipe, came out onto the stage.

"Mr. House," said the announcer, "before you begin, can we impose upon you to display your remarkable powers of deduction for the audience?"

"Certainly," said Sherringford House. "May I have a volunteer, please?"

Well, I could see right off that there weren't going to be no sinners on display, so I got up to leave.

"Thank you, sir," said House, and suddenly everyone started staring at me.

"You talking to me?" I said.

"You have recently been in Paris, I perceive," he said, "and I believe it is not incorrect to state that you toil in the service of your Lord."

"Now how on earth did you know that?" I asked.

He merely smiled, and suddenly everyone started applauding.

"The science of deduction," he said after they'd all calmed down, "can be divided into three separate parts: observation, analysis, and conclusion. Anyone who has been properly trained can do what I just did. You ask how I have solved one hundred and three cases without a failure, and I say to you that had the police learned those three basic principles—observation, analysis, and conclusion—they would not have needed my services in any of them."

"Rubbish!" said a voice from the audience.

"I beg your pardon?" said House.

"I say that's balderdash, and that you're a fake," said the voice, which was suddenly sounding pretty familiar. "What's more, I'm willing to bet five thousand pounds that I can prove it."

"Please stand up, sir, so that I may see you," said House.

The man stood up, and now that I could get a good look at him, I realized that it was Erich Von Horst.

"I will put a challenge to you, Mr. House," said Von Horst. "In three nights' time, I will steal the Crown Jewels, and I'll wager five thousand pounds that you and the entire London Metropolitan Police Force cannot prevent me from so doing."

"Arrest that criminal!" shouted a woman.

"No!" said House sharply. "This man has challenged my integrity. Were I to back down, I would be less than British, which is unthinkable." He turned back to Von Horst. "Sir," he said, "have you any conditions attached to your challenge?"

"I will need one assistant," said Von Horst.

"Professor Melanoma, perhaps?" said House, arching an eyebrow sardonically.

"I need no one else to help me plan the theft," said Von Horst. "To prove it, I will accept someone from the audience, if you will promise that he or she will not be prosecuted."

"That is acceptable," said House. "I will speak to Inspector McIlvoy, and I'm sure he will agree." He paused. "Who do you choose?"

Von Horst looked straight at me and smiled. "It makes no difference," he said. "It might as well be the gentleman from Paris."

"Done, sir," said House. He now turned to the announcer. "Will you be good enough to hold the stakes?"

"Gladly, Mr. House," replied the announcer. House pulled out a checkbook and began scribbling while Von Horst approached the stage and handed over a huge wad of bills.

"It does not bother you that I have seen your face?" asked House.

"Not in the least," said Von Horst confidently, "for you shall never see it again."

"Ladies and gentlemen," said House, "I hope you will forgive me, but I must postpone this lecture while I prepare to apprehend this villain. If the management will agree, your tickets will be honored for a week from tonight, at which time I shall tell you exactly how I captured him and saved the Crown Jewels."

That brought a standing ovation, and then House walked off the stage and everyone except Von Horst started filing out.

"Good evening, Doctor Jones," said Von Horst when we were alone in the theater. "Fancy meeting you here, of all places. What a small world it is."

"Crowded is more the word for it," I said bitterly.

"Ah," he said. "You're still mad about our little venture in Italy."

"You might say that."

"Then this is my chance to put things right between us," he said. "I'll let you in for one third."

"Things ain't been right between us since the day I first met you back in Dar es Salaam, and they didn't get no better in Morocco or Algeria or Mozambique or Italy. Just get out of my life."

"What kind of attitude is that for a man of the cloth?" he said. "How can I atone for my past sins if you turn your back on me?"

"Von Horst," I said, "there's probably a couple of hundred things I might do to you, but turning my back on you ain't one of 'em."

"How can I prove my sincerity?" he said. "I have a foolproof plan to steal the Crown Jewels. I'm so sure it will work that I put up five thousand pounds against the greatest detective in the world. You will be working for me. You'll know all the details of my plan, the location of my headquarters, everything you need to turn me in if you should decide that I'm trying to deceive you in any way. Furthermore, Sherringford House has given his personal guarantee that you will not be held culpable if I succeed. What more could you possibly want?"

"Everything always *sounds* good when you lay it out," I said, "but somehow or other you always get the money and I always wind up in the hoosegow."

"But you *can't* wind up in jail this time!" he said. "If I'm caught, you go scot-free, and if I succeed, you get a third of the Crown Jewels."

I mulled on it for a couple of minutes.

"What makes you so sure you can outwit Sherringford House?" I said. "Even *I've* heard of him, and I ain't never been in England before today."

"Doctor Jones," he said, "this plan simply cannot fail. I don't care how brilliant House is, I don't care if the Tower of London is entirely surrounded by police, I will come away with the Crown Jewels." He paused. "And the beauty of the scheme is that it requires no special skills whatsoever. I don't have to be able to climb up the sides of buildings or pick complex combination locks or fight my way past an army of policemen. It took a genius to conceive it, but any fool could carry it out."

It was at that very instant that my own plan occurred to me. If any fool could carry out the theft of the Crown Jewels, well, I could be every bit as much of a fool as the next man. I figured that I'd go along with him until I learned all the details of his scheme. Then I'd tell House just enough so he'd be waiting for Von Horst, and while he was carting Von Horst off to the calaboose, I'd use the plan to help myself to a couple of generous handfuls of the Crown Jewels and finally get around to building me a tabernacle worthy of my preaching talents.

"Well," said Von Horst, "what do you say? Are you in or out?"

"In."

"Good," he said. "I *knew* I could count on you. And you won't regret it."

"Actually, I got a good feeling about this here enterprise," I allowed. "Like you said, there's no way I can lose."

"Shall we shake on it?" he asked.

"Just a minute," I said, slipping off my watch and putting it on my left wrist. "Okay."

"Somehow I have the feeling you still don't entirely trust me, Doctor Jones," he said, shaking my hand.

"Maybe I will after you explain your plan to me," I said.

"Fair enough," he agreed. "But not here. There's too much chance that we'll be overheard." He looked around. "Do you know the Garroted Goose?"

"It's a kid's nursery rhyme, right?"

"It's a pub on Bond Street. Be there at noon tomorrow."

He turned and walked out of the theater, and a minute later I hunted up a phone book and found Sherringford House's address, and half an hour after that I was introducing myself to his landlady, who showed me up the steps to his apartment. I heard fiddle music coming through the door, and commented that it sounded right pretty.

"Oh, Mr. House is a great one for the violin," said the landlady. "The house is filled with music whenever he's thinking."

"He thinks a lot, does he?" I asked.

"Practically all the time," she said. Then she whispered, "Just between us, I do wish he'd vary the melody every now and then." We reached the landing. "Well, here we are. It's the first door to your left."

"Do come in," said House's voice, just before I could knock on the door.

"Howdy, Mr. House," I said, entering his apartment, which was filled with books and chemicals in equal proportion.

"Ah, the gentleman from the theater," he said, turning off his Victrola and putting the record back in its package. "Please sit down."

"Thank you," I said, pulling up a chair.

"You have come to me because of the proposed burglary of the Crown Jewels, have you not?" he said.

"Yeah," I said. "How did you know that?"

An amused smile crossed his face. "What other business could we possibly have to discuss?"

"Well, it seems simple when you explain it," I said, "but for the life of me, I still don't know how you figured out I had just got here from Paris and was in the service of the Lord."

"Elementary," he said. "On the sole of your left shoe there remains a trace of horse manure. Beneath your fingernails is the sort of grime that is most easily accrued by working with animals. Your accent is American. Your bearing and demeanor is something less than aristocratic, and I therefore deduce that far from being a sportsman you are a common laborer. Now, where would an American be most likely to find work on a horse farm? In Paris, Kentucky, the breeding capital of the thoroughbred industry. And why would you suddenly come to England? Because Lord Pemberton has only this week moved his racing operation from the Blue Grass country to Britain, and since he is well known for rewarding loyalty in his employees, it stands to reason that he has relocated all of his American help here in London. Therefore, it was a simple matter to conclude that you have recently arrived from Paris, and that you remain in the service of your Lord." He leaned back and puffed smugly on his pipe.

"Well, if that don't beat all!" I said.

"It's nothing," he said, getting to his feet. "Let me observe you further for a moment."

I sat still like I was posing for a picture, until he walked once around me, nodded his head, and plumped himself back down on the sofa.

"You are left handed, your mother died during childbirth, you are a crack shot with a .38 caliber revolver, and your fondest desire is to translate Shakespeare into Serbo-Croatian."

"Truth to tell," I said, "I'm right handed, last time I heard from my mother she was serving hard time in Colorado for running a bawdy house, I ain't never shot a pistol in my life, and my fondest desire is to raise enough money to build the Tabernacle of Saint Luke."

"Well," he said with a shrug, "it had to be one or the other." He took another puff of his pipe. "And now, what can I do for you, Mr...?"

"Reverend," I said. "The Right Reverend Doctor Lucifer Jones."

"Doctor?" he said, suddenly alert. "I don't suppose you'd have access to...well, no, never mind. Please continue."

"Well, Mr. House," I said, "I been a law-abiding citizen and a God-fearing Christian all my life, and I just don't feel right helping Erich Von Horst steal the Crown Jewels out from under your nose, so to speak, and while I appreciate the fact that no one's going to arrest me no matter what happens, I'd feel a lot better about things if I knew I was helping to uphold the law rather than bust it."

"A most commendable attitude," he said.

"So I got to thinking on it," I continued, "and I figured that the very best thing to do would be to find out exactly what Von Horst's plan is, and to pass it on to you so you'd be ready and waiting for him."

"Well, I thank you very much for your concern, Reverend Jones," said House, "but it would hardly be sporting, now that we've made our bet."

"What's sporting got to do with anything?" I said. "This man has stolen and finagled his way all up and down Africa without getting caught, and now he's going after the Crown Jewels."

"Africa?" he said with a laugh. "Not a chance, Reverend Jones. I studied him carefully when he came up to the stage, and I can tell you with total confidence that he has spent the last seventeen years as a bookkeeper in Brisbane, Australia. He is henpecked by his wife, devoted to his seven children—two boys and five girls—and spends his Sundays watching cricket matches from a seat that faces north-northeast."

"I tell you he swindled his way across the length and breadth of Africa," I said.

"Poor fellow," he said sympathetically. "I fear that when that horse kicked you in the head last November—or was it October? No, November—it must have jarred loose some of your memory."

"Can we just agree that wherever he's been, he's here now, and the main thing is to stop him from stealing the Crown Jewels?"

"Certainly," said House. "And prevent him I shall."

"Wouldn't it be a lot easier if you knew his plan?" I asked him.

House shot me a confident smile. "But I already do," he said.

"You do?"

"Certainly," he said. "The man is obviously a master of disguise. At precisely eleven o'clock three nights hence, when they change the guards in front of the jewel room, he will present himself for duty, dressed as a sergeant in the Tower Guard. He will take his post outside the door, snap to attention, and patiently wait for us to lose interest in him and direct our attention elsewhere on the assumption that he has not yet gained access to the Tower. Then, when the corridor is deserted, he will dispatch his fellow guard with a single blow to the back of the neck—the man is obviously an expert at karate; brown belt, I should think—and will enter the jewel room, prepared to make off with millions of pounds of Britain's greatest treasures. But I, Sherringford House, will be hidden inside that room, waiting for him."

"Well, that sure sounds like you got it figured out," I said. "But if you're right, what does he need *me* for?"

"In case the police remain in the vicinity of the jewel room after he has taken up his position, he will need you to create a commotion on one of the lower levels, drawing the police away so that he can have a few necessary moments alone to perpetrate his foul crime." He paused and relit his pipe, which kept going out. "It is a brilliant scheme, as he said it was, and it is indeed almost foolproof. He forgot to take only one single factor into consideration."

"Yeah?" I said. "And what was that?"

"He forgot that he would be trying to fool the greatest consulting detective in the world," said House, who sure wasn't weighted down by no false modesty. "So you see, Reverend Jones, the situation is already well in hand. I thank you for your concern, but Von Horst will be in jail before the Tower clock strikes midnight three days hence."

"You're absolutely sure you ain't made a mistake?" I said.

"A mistake?" he said. "*Me?*"

Well, I could see we didn't have nothing more to talk about, so I took my leave of him and wandered on back to Basil Street. I woke up about ten in the morning, found out that nobody in London knew how to make a good cup of coffee, and when it was getting on toward noon I moseyed over to the Garroted Goose, where Von Horst was waiting for me at a table in the back.

"Good morning, Doctor Jones," he said. "I trust you slept well?"

"Passably," I said. "I had a pretty comfortable room, except maybe for the bed and the mattress and the springs and the pillow."

"Well, three days from now, you can stay in the Royal Suite at the Dorchester," he said. Suddenly he grinned. "And Sherringford House will never even know he's been bested!"

"You keep saying that," I pointed out, "but you don't say *how*."

"I'm about to," said Von Horst. "Have you been to the Tower of London yet, Doctor Jones?"

"Nope," I said. "I thought I'd take a gander at it this afternoon."

"Well, when you do, you will see that the jewels are kept in a heavily guarded room at the very top of the Tower," said Von Horst. "There are guards on duty around the clock, the door has a lock that it said to be unbreakable, and the only way down is by a single staircase. Every great thief in the history of crime has attempted to steal the Crown Jewels," he added, "but none has ever succeeded—until now."

"If I was a betting man, I'd go with the run," I said.

"Ah—but I know something that even Sherringford House doesn't know," said Von Horst with a grin.

"Yeah?"

He nodded. "Most of the jewels on display in the Tower are fake. The *real* jewels are locked away in a vault below ground level—and *that* vault can be cracked. The government has no desire to call attention to it, so it is not guarded, not marked in any way, and indeed looks like any storage room. While House and the police are waiting in the Tower, I shall be directly below them, where I will have all night to steal the unprotected Crown Jewels at my leisure."

"You *sure* of this?" I asked.

"Would I have bet five thousand pounds if I had any doubts?" replied Von Horst. "I got it from an embittered woman who once thought she had a chance to marry Edward and become the Queen of all England. He toyed with her affections and then left her, and for years she has been nursing her bitterness and waiting for her revenge. It was after we were introduced by a mutual friend and I admitted some of my youthful indiscretions to her that she decided to impart this knowledge to me, in the hope that after I had accomplished my mission I would make it public and thus make fools of the entire Royal Family." He smiled. "And what better way to publicize it than to defeat and humiliate England's favorite son, Sherringford House?"

"Just where do *I* enter into these here plans?" I said.

"You must convince House that, for some unfathomable reason, you have taken a strong dislike to me and wish to thwart me. You will give him some cock-and-bull story that we will concoct about how I plan to sneak into the jewel room, so that all his efforts are concentrated there, and he never realizes that while he is waiting for me, I have arrived and stolen the *real* jewels directly below where he is standing."

"And that's it?" I asked.

"That's it," he said. "What do you think?"

What I thought was that he'd be out of the country with the jewels while I was stuck in the Tower and he had never had any intention of paying me my one third, but I just grinned at him and said, "You were right; it sounds foolproof to me."

"I'm staying at the Savoy," he said. "Come by tomorrow night and we'll work out the bogus plan that you can relate to House and which will keep all his efforts and attentions confined to the Tower."

"What time?" I asked.

"Shall we say eight o'clock?" suggested Von Horst. "We could do it sooner, of course, but I want House to think it took me a full two days to confide in you. It seems more realistic this way."

I got up and told him that I'd see him the next night. Then I went right to a bookstore and bought a map of the Tower of London. The real jewel room wasn't on it, but I found the stairs leading down to its level, and it looked like Von Horst had figured things out pretty well. There were plenty of escape routes, and if things got really tense, he could open a window and just jump into the Thames. In fact, it was such a good plan that I decided I'd keep it for myself.

I spent the rest of the day getting my first good look at London, which was real long and strong on museums and stuff, but right short on gambling houses. I figured I might take in a little culture, so I went to a theater in the evening, but instead of moving pictures they had a bunch of real live people on stage. Still, it was a pretty entertaining comedy, and when this here prince started talking to a skull, of all things, I broke right out laughing, which led me to the realization that Londoners ain't got no sense of humor because everyone else just turned and stared at me and began trying to shush me up, so I got up, real dignified like, and walked out, feeling right sorry for all them poor actors who were probably wondering why no one else appreciated all their jokes.

The next day I slept til noon, and figured I'd spend the day at the races, so I asked the desk clerk where I could find Ascot and Epsom, and he gave me two addresses, but evidently he didn't understand plain spoken American real good, because the first address turned out to be a men's clothing shop and the second was a druggist, and all I had to show for my hopeful afternoon at the track was an Ascot tie and a box of Epsom salts.

I stopped at a local restaurant and had what they assured me was a typical British dinner, which led me to understand why I kept running into expatriate Brits all over the world. The lemonade could have used a little sugar to make up for not having no lemons, and with no ketchup to bring out the subtle nuances of flavor in the Dover sole, I decided they sold the leftovers to cobblers who had appropriated the word for shoe bottoms.

When it was getting on toward eight o'clock I went over to the Savoy, and found out from the desk clerk that Von Horst was in room 533 and was expecting me, so I took the elevator up to the fifth floor and began walking down the hall. Just as I passed room 531 I thought I could hear Von Horst's voice, and as I walked up to his door I could hear him, plain as day, speaking on the telephone.

"Yes, it's all working out beautifully," he said. "The man is a complete and total fool. By now he has doubtless decided to alert Sherringford House to what he believes is my true plan, and to appropriate it for himself at some time in the future." He chuckled at something, and then continued. "No, there's no way it can fail. Half the London police will be in the Tower, and the rest will be watching the storage room, and while they are all occupied, *I* shall sneak into Buckingham Palace and steal all the jewels they have taken out for the King of Norway's state dinner. I never did say *which* Crown Jewels I planned to steal, and while they're watching one set, I'll make off with the other and deliver them to you before sunrise…You'll have to sit on them for a couple of years, but since I'm only asking thirty percent of market value, I think it's fair to say that we'll both make out like, shall we say, thieves?"

He laughed again, and I knocked on his door.

"I'll be right with you!" he yelled, and then I heard him say into the telephone, "I have to hang up now. You won't hear from me again until after the job is done."

Then I heard him walk across the room, and the door opened, and he greeted me with a great big smile.

"Good evening, Doctor Jones," he said. "I'm sorry if I kept you waiting, but I was in the lavatory."

"Quite all right," I said, walking in and sitting myself down in a leather chair. "Quite a spread you've got here."

"It's cozy," he agreed. "Can I get you anything to drink?"

I allowed as to how a glass of whiskey might wash away the taste of a typical British dinner, and he poured some for each of us, and then he sat down opposite me and while I finished my drink he instructed me to tell Sherringford House that he planned to impersonate a Tower Guard and have me create a commotion on the lower levels, and that when House and the police went down below to investigate he would disable the other guard with a karate chop, pick the lock, and steal the jewels before anyone returned.

"It's the stupidest scheme in the world," he said with a chuckle. "But I've been reading House's adventures in the magazines, and he's just dumb enough to buy it."

"Yeah," I said. "I'll bet I could get him to go for it."

"Your job," he added, "is to lead them a merry chase without ever going below ground level, where I'll be stealing the real jewels from the storeroom. Do you think you can manage it?"

"I can't see why not," I said.

"Fine. We'll meet at Westminster Abbey at four in the morning, where I'll give you your share of the jewels."

"Fair enough," I said agreeably.

"All right," he said, getting to his feet. "Is there anything else we have to discuss?"

"Not that I can think of."

"Good. Then I'll see you approximately thirty-two hours from now, at which point we should both join the ranks of Britain's richest men."

I walked on back to my hotel and sat down and started mulling on everything I had heard. Obviously Von Horst was using his bet just to divert the attention of Sherringford House and the London police so that he could have a clear, unhindered shot at all the jewels in Buckingham Palace, and I had known all along he planned to double-cross me, though I didn't know until I overheard his phone call exactly how he planned to do it.

So I got to sorting things out, and it seemed to me that since House already believed in Von Horst's phony scheme even though I hadn't yet told it to him, there wasn't no sense at all disappointing him, so I would lay it out just the way Von Horst wanted me to, and that would take care of the world's greatest consulting detective and the whole of the London Metropolitan Police Force.

Then, since I knew that the gems at Buckingham Palace would be unprotected, and that Von Horst had arranged everything so that he could sneak in and steal them at eleven o'clock, all I had to do was get there ahead of him, at maybe 10:30, and once I'd gotten safely back to my hotel I could call the Tower and tell 'em Von Horst was lurking in the Palace grounds, and that would take care of him once and for all, since he'd publicly promised to steal the jewels and they would sure as shootin' get themselves stolen.

The more I thought about it, the more I couldn't see no way it could go wrong, so finally I moseyed over to House's apartment and told him that he was dead right about what Von Horst planned to do.

"Was there ever any doubt?" he said with a contented smile.

"Then, if it's all the same to you, I'd rather not be anywhere on the premises, since Von Horst has a pretty vile temper and I don't want him taking no pot shots at me when he finds out I spilled the beans."

"Certainly," said House. "Your job is done, Reverend Jones. I commend you for your citizenship and your service to the Crown, though of course I knew all along what Von Horst was planning, as you'll recall from our conversation two nights ago."

He walked me to the door and bid me good night, and then I went back to Bristol Street, and spent the rest of the night and most of the next day resting up. I knew better than to try another British home-cooked dinner again, so I went out in search of a healthy meal and got myself two egg rolls, a chocolate donut, and a stein of ale, and at ten o'clock I started walking over to Buckingham Palace.

When I got there I saw that the whole building was dark, and I figured that all the kings and queens and aristocrats were indulging in their party games a little early, and that I might have to go from one bedroom to another collecting their treasures, but I'd brung a flashlight along with me, so that didn't bother me none. I walked up to one of the back windows, and since I didn't want to make no noise, I took off my shoes and then climbed in.

I found myself in some kind of drawing room, and since it was empty I opened the door and walked out into a huge corridor, and started opening doors and inspecting rooms one by one, but I couldn't find no jewelry or people or nothing in 'em, and after a few minutes I was beginning to wonder if maybe there was more than one Buckingham Palace, and if Edward and all the royal folks was in the other one and this one was owned by a kindly old couple named Buckingham who were asleep on the second floor.

Finally I made it to the living room, which was maybe a hundred feet long and half as wide, and I figured that if there wasn't no gems to be had, maybe I could at least pick up a knick knack or two so it wouldn't be a totally wasted evening, and just as I was reaching for a little statue of a lady who was dressed as if she'd just stepped out of a shower and didn't have no towels nearby, all the lights came on and a voice shouted "You're under arrest!" and suddenly I was facing four hundred members of the London police.

"What are you guys doing here?" I asked. "You're supposed to be over at the Tower of London."

"We had a tip that someone would try to rob Buckingham while the Royal Family was vacationing at Windsor Castle," said the officer in charge.

"Well, somebody *is* gonna try to rob the Palace," I said, "and if you'll just stick around a few minutes you can catch him red-handed."

"We just did," said the officer with a laugh.

"You got it all wrong," I said. "I'm the Right Reverend Doctor Lucifer Jones. Don't that mean nothing to you?"

"It means you'll probably be thrown out of your church when they find out what you were doing," he said.

"But you can't arrest me!" I said. "I got an agreement with Sherringford House!"

"Sure you do," said the officer. "Now put your hands behind your back."

"But I do!" I said as they slipped on a set of handcuffs. "Just ask him."

"Sherringford House is much too busy protecting the Crown Jewels to be bothered right now," said the officer.

And that was that. They led me off to the British version of a paddywagon and took me to the local station and photographed and fingerprinted me and booked me and locked me in a cell just like a common criminal. They even took away my cigars and my hip flask and my personal pair of custom-made dice, and left me with nothing but my well-worn copy of the Good Book, which wasn't as comforting as it might have been, since it was too dark to read or swat flies with it.

Well, I finally drifted off to sleep, and in the morning who should show up but Sherringford House. He nodded to the guard, who unlocked my cell.

"I'm terribly sorry for this misunderstanding," said the consulting detective. "You are, of course, free to go. The London police have agreed to honor my promise to you."

"Thanks," I said.

"It was the least I could do for you," he said, "considering that I won the five thousand pounds."

"You caught Von Horst?" I said, surprised.

He shook his head. "He never showed up. At the very last minute he must have realized that he could never hope to elude Sherringford House." He turned to me and shook my hand. "It has been most interesting working with you, Reverend Jones. I hope you enjoy the remainder of your stay in London."

He walked off, and I went over to the desk to pick up my belongings.

"You're Lucifer Jones?" asked the desk sergeant.

"The Right Reverend Lucifer Jones," I corrected him.

"Here's your gear," he said, handing me a small cardboard box. "And this letter was hand-delivered for you about an hour ago."

I opened it up and read it.

My Dear Doctor Jones:

Once again I have found collaborating with you to be a stimulating and enriching experience. I had been planning to steal the Crown jewels for almost a month, but I had to wait until the perfect partner showed up, so you can imagine my elation when I saw you walking into Sherringford House's lecture three nights ago.

After I had arranged the wager and convinced you to join forces with me, I knew it would only be a matter of time before you betrayed me and tried to steal the jewels yourself. I also knew that House would have most of the London Metropolitan Police Force gathered at the Tower. The trick, of course, was to let you overhear me talking to myself as you approached my room at the Savoy, because I knew that the police would hold a few men in reserve to protect the rest of the city, and I had to find some way to get them all in one place, far from where the actual crime was being committed.

That is where you came in, Doctor Jones. Once you heard me say that I would be stealing the jewels from the Palace at eleven, I knew that I could count on two things: first, that you would keep this information to yourself and not divulge it to Sherringford House, and second, that you would show up sometime before eleven to rob the jewels yourself.

It only took a phone call to the police to alert them to the fact that someone would be breaking into the Palace between ten and eleven—and while they were apprehending you and Sherringford House was wasting his time in the Tower of London, I was free to commit the robbery that I had planned from the beginning.

If you will walk over to Bond Street after reading this letter, you will find a jewelry store owned by a Mr. Alastair Crown. Prior to last night, he had the Moons of Africa, three perfectly matched diamonds, on display in his window. They are now in my possession, and by the time you read this I will be out of the country.

As for the five thousand pounds, if you can convince House that he lost his wager, I happily forfeit all claim to it and gladly give it to you. It was a small enough investment, considering that it resulted in my acquiring some three million dollars' worth of diamonds.

I realize that you may feel ill-used, but the fact of the matter is that I told both you and House the truth: I did in fact steal the Crown jewels exactly when I said I would do so. If you don't believe me, just ask Mr. Crown, who must be somewhat distraught at this moment and could doubtless use such spiritual comfort as a man of the cloth such as yourself might wish to bring him.

Yr. Obdt. Svt.,

Erich Von Horst

I crumpled up the letter and threw it on the floor, and then went out into the wilderness—which in this case happened to be a bench in Hyde Park—and had a long heart-to-heart with my Silent

Partner, and we decided to pull up stakes and try our luck in some other municipality since we hadn't done all that well since arriving in London.

Then He went off to tend to other Godly business and left me to wonder why, where Erich Von Horst was concerned, I could be so stupid when I am so smart.

9. THE LOCH NESS MONSTER

I hopped a northbound train out of London, got involved in a friendly little game of chance with three of the conductors, and when I looked up we were not only out of England but had left Glasgow far behind us. I figured the next stop was probably the North Pole, but one of the conductors assured me that the train didn't go no farther than Inverness, which was plenty far enough as far as I was concerned, since I hadn't never heard of it.

Well, let me tell you, Inverness ain't one of the glittering capitals of Europe—or even of Scotland, if push comes to shove. One of the locals suggested I stay at Culloden House, which he told me was right where Bonnie Prince Charlie had been defeated, so I moseyed over and rented a room, but I couldn't find hide nor hair of no prince, so I reckoned he'd given up whatever fight he'd been in and gone on home to lick his wounds.

The chambermaid was a girl named Anna, whose father worked as the gamekeeper for the local laird who owned most of the nearby property, and we hit it off right quick for two people who didn't have much in common—I liked women and she hankered after men. It was after our idyllic little tryst that I asked her what the locals did to amuse themselves, which seemed like a perfectly innocent and harmless thing to ask, but her only response was to climb out of the bed and throw a lamp at me. I took this as a gentle reproof to the way I had worded my question, but after she threw a chair and both my shoes at me I could see that she was mildly displeased, so I simply thanked her for showing a stranger some of the brighter glories of Scotland and allowed that I would mosey on down to the local tavern and see if anyone there was more of a mind to direct me to such action as might be taking place in Inverness of a Tuesday evening.

Due to my little interlude with Anna, it was getting on toward midnight when I reached the tavern, and there weren't more than half a dozen old men sitting around, all staring at this great big clock over the bar. There were a bunch of nasty-looking fish mounted on the walls, with little metal plaques saying who caught them and when, and here and there were photos of some Brit wearing a crown, which I thought was probably King Edward but I didn't want to ask, just in case it turned out to be this Prince Charlie and he still had friends in the vicinity.

"Good evening, stranger," said the bartender. "I haven't seen you here before."

"I just got into town today," I said, and since everyone was looking at me, I turned to face 'em. "The Right Reverend Honorable Doctor Lucifer Jones at your service, weddings and baptisms done cheap, with a group rate for funerals."

"Pleased to meet you, Reverend Jones," said the bartender. "And since you're a man of the cloth, the first one will be on the house."

"Well, that's right generous of you, brother," I said. "All them millions of people who swear the Scots are a mean, stingy, miserly race of tightwads obviously ain't been to Inverness lately."

"Thank you," said the bartender. "I think."

"You plan on being here long, Reverend Jones?" asked one of the old guys who was sitting alone at a table.

"I doubt it," I said. "Three of four hours of hard drinking and I ought to be ready for bed."

"I meant, do you plan to stay in Inverness for any length of time?"

"I ain't made up my mind yet," I said. "I've spent the last few years wandering the world, looking for the right spot for me and God to build our tabernacle."

"Just getting the lay of the land, eh?"

Well, I thought I'd already *got* the lay of the land with Anna back at Culloden House, but it seemed ungentlemanly to mention it to strangers, at least until they started bragging about what *they'd* caught lately, so I just kind of nodded in agreement.

"If there's anything we can do to help, places to point out, things like that, just let us know," he said.

"Well, as long as you're being so open and honest to a newcomer, what do you fellers do for excitement of a weekday evening?" I asked.

He looked around. "Should we tell him?"

The others all stared at me, and one by one they nodded.

"First," he said, turning back to me, "you have to promise not to tell anyone."

"You got my word as a man of the cloth," I said.

"All right," he said. "After midnight, when the constable's gone to sleep, and the laird and his gamekeeper are all locked up in their castle for the night, we sneak over to the Loch and poach salmon."

Well, if poaching salmon was their idea of a good time, I could see that Inverness wasn't the most wide-open town I'd ever been to. Personally, I couldn't see that it was any more exciting than poaching eggs, which is also not the most thrilling sport in the world, and I couldn't figure out why they had to wait until the constable and all them other people were asleep, unless there was some law on the books that the only way you could cook salmon was to fry or broil it, but it occurred to me that I hadn't eaten since I got off the train and that a little poached salmon on toast might just hit the spot, so I asked if I could tag along.

"Are you sure you want to get involved in this, Reverend?" asked one of the men.

"Why not?" I said.

"Isn't it against your religion?"

"Show me in the Good Book where it says you can't poach salmon in Inverness," I replied.

"Reverend Jones," said one of the men, getting up and putting an arm around my shoulders, "I *like* your brand of Christianity. You build your tabernacle, and you've got your first customer in Angus McNair."

We had a couple of more drinks, and then Angus McNair decided it was time to go poach the salmon, and we wandered out of the tavern and walked through town, and then we started going across some bog outside of town, and just as I was wondering why we couldn't have used a kitchen that was a little closer, we came to this great big lake.

"Here we are, Reverend," said McNair.

"You're gonna poach the salmon right here?" I asked.

"Couldn't very well poach it back in town, could we?" he said, and everyone laughed, so just to be polite I laughed too, though for the life of me I couldn't figure out why not, unless they figured it tasted better over an open fire.

"Let's get the boats out," said McNair, and suddenly they pushed back a bunch of dead branches and brought out three boats. "You can come with me, Reverend Jones."

"We're going out on the lake?" I said.

"Unless you feel like rowing on dry land," he replied.

Well, I didn't have no answer to that, so I just climbed in alongside of him, and we rowed out to where the current was mighty swift, and then he tossed a net over the side, and rowed back to shore hell for leather, and once we got there he climbed out and started gathering in the net, and there were four or five big salmon in it, and I noticed both of the other boats had done the same and were gathering in their own salmon.

By this time I was hungry enough to eat one raw, but I decided that I might as well be polite and wait til they got around to poaching 'em.

"Ain't you gonna build no fire?" I asked.

"And alert the constable and the gamekeeper?" said McNair. "The whole reason we come here after midnight is to *avoid* them."

"What *are* you going to do, then?" I asked.

"We'll chop off their heads and gut them, and then bring them back to the village."

"I don't want to appear unduly forward," I said, "but does anyone ever get around to actually eating 'em?"

"Certainly," said McNair. "We'll feast tomorrow, eh, men?"

The others all chuckled and nodded, which left me to wondering what we were doing there tonight, but I didn't want to say nothing that would make me appear ignorant, so I just kept my mouth shut and watched while they went to work on the salmon. They tossed all the heads and guts into a big metal pail, and then McNair handed it to me.

"Here," he said. "Toss this into the loch, and be careful."

I walked to the edge of the water, and suddenly I heard a bunch of birds screeching and squawking and looked to see what the commotion was all about, but there wasn't nothing happening, so I turned back to the water, all prepared to dump the pail, when I found myself face to face with something that was awfully green and mighty wet and plenty big and mostly scary.

"Give it to her quick, Reverend," said McNair, "before she decides to take it right out of your hand."

This here creature was maybe a couple of hundred feet long, and covered with scales, and it kind of reached out this enormous neck until its head was hovering right over me, and if its face was nothing to write home about, let me tell you that its breath was even worse.

I tossed what I was holding, pail and all, at the creature's face, and it just opened up its mouth and swallowed, and after I finished counting its teeth I looked down its throat and decided there was plenty of room for a man of the cloth to slide right down without causing no serious problems at all, so I did what any reasonable man would do and raced back to the boats like unto an Olympic sprinter.

"What the hell was *that*?" I asked.

"Ah, that was only Nessie," said McNair with a shrug.

"There wasn't nothing *only* about it!" I said. "If I didn't know better, I'd swear I just saw a sea serpent!"

"You did," answered McNair. "You've heard of the Loch Ness Monster?"

"As has been writ up in song and story?" I asked.

He nodded. "This is Loch Ness, and that was the monster." He paused and looked at the ripples in the water, which were the only sign that a monster had recently come around begging for table scraps. "We get dozens of scientists out here every year, looking for her, but old Nessie, she's got an aversion to people. Only time she ever breaks the surface is when she knows we're going to throw her the leftovers from our salmon poaching."

Which was precisely the moment that my hunger for a little poached salmon got itself overtook by my hunger for a little easy money.

"You mean all you got to do is come to the lake here, and go out on your boats, and she knows you're going to toss her some fish guts?" I asked.

"That's pretty much the way it works," agreed McNair.

"And as long as you feed her, she don't never molest you, or breathe smoke and fire, or gobble up your boats, or nothing antisocial like that?" I continued.

"She's a nice old girl, Nessie is," said McNair. "We don't bother her, she don't bother us. The way we see it, the salmon innards and heads are her commission for letting us fish in her loch."

"Well, that's right interesting, Brother McNair," I said. "And you say she don't never show herself to the august members of the scientific community?"

"Nope," he said. "She's got no more use for 'em than we have."

"There wouldn't be any such members around here, would there?" I asked.

"I hear tell there's an American staying over at Glen Mohr," he said with a chuckle. "Been on the loch for two weeks now. I believe he's due to stay here for another week before he goes home and tells all his peers that the monster is just a myth."

Just about that time one of McNair's colleagues pulled out a hip flask, and we all had a little nip to keep the cold night air at bay, and then we went back across the bog to Inverness, and while they all went to sleep, I lay on my bed in Culloden House and tried to see where the most likely profit was to be had from the monster's existence.

I figured that no scientist, no matter how gullible, would pay me good coin of the realm to lead them to Nessie until they knew beyond a doubt that she existed, but if they saw her, then they didn't need *me* to prove it to them. I mulled on it til daybreak, and as I was having breakfast the solution finally dawned on me: I would buy a camera and take some pictures of Nessie, and once I showed them to the scientist, he'd be more than willing to pay me a finder's fee for leading him to her.

I hadn't never taken a picture in my life, but as soon as the stores opened I picked me up a camera and half a dozen rolls of film. Anna was feeling a little less angry in the light of day, so I had her show me how to work the shutter and apertures and such, and just to make sure I had the hang of it, I took a practice roll of her standing on the front porch of the hotel.

Then I stopped by a fish market, of which there were an awful lot in Inverness, bought a bunch of heads and guts that the owner was going to throw out, stuck 'em in a pail, tried not to notice the smell as I carted it off to Loch Ness, and went out in Angus McNair's boat. I spent a few minutes on the lake, then rowed to shore and waited—and sure enough, Nessie showed up a minute later, all two hundred hungry feet of her, and I took a whole roll of film of her gobbling up the fish heads and innards I had laid out all nice and neat on a log between me and her. Then she belched once, and disappeared beneath the surface of the water.

I stopped by the camera store, gave him all my exposed film to develop, and went back to Culloden House, where I tried to catch up on my sleep and Anna tried to catch up on her romancing, and though it was a near thing, I got 'em both done in the proper order.

I just kind of loafed around the next day, and in mid-afternoon I stopped by and picked up my pictures. Everything had come out clear as you like, and I decided that if I ever gave up preaching, I could probably make a living taking artistic photographs of ladies in their unmentionables for use in calendars and other such vital publications.

First thing the next morning, I left a package of Anna's photos with her and told her to send 'em to her father with my compliments, just so he'd know a new and thoughtful preacher had set up shop in town. I passed Angus McNair and his cronies coming back from a hard night's fishing as I moseyed over to Glen Mohr, which was an old Tudor house that had been turned into a hotel, and I sat myself down in the lobby and waited until the guests started moving around. Finally a young feller with thick glasses and bushy hair walked down the stairs, said good morning to the desk clerk in perfect American, and headed off for the dining room, and I got up and followed him.

"Excuse me," I said, walking up to him once he'd been seated. "But I'm the Right Reverend Doctor Lucifer Jones, out of Moline, Illinois. I been preaching my way across the world for close to a dozen years now, and hearing your accent made me realize just how much I miss the green hills of home."

"There aren't any hills in Illinois," he said.

"But if there were, they'd sure be green, wouldn't they?" I said. "Anyway, I'd be happy to buy you breakfast in exchange for the pleasure of talking to a fellow Yank after all this time."

"Well, that's a different matter," said the man. "Pull up a chair and join me, Reverend Jones."

"Glad to," I said, sitting down opposite him. "You up here to do a little fishing?"

"No," said the man. "My name is Norbert Nelson. I'm a scientist, here to collect data on the Loch Ness Monster."

"No kidding?" I said. "What have you collected so far?"

"About three hundred mosquito bites and a bad cold," said Nelson. "But at least I'm on the verge of proving conclusively that the monster doesn't exist."

"Yeah?"

He nodded. "I'm due to stay another five days, but as far as I'm concerned, I might as well pack up and go home now. I can't imagine where this monster myth got started, but there isn't any basis for it."

"What a shame," I said, shaking my head. "I suppose finding the monster could have made you rich and famous?"

"Well, let's put it this way, Reverend Jones," said Nelson with a smile. "I'll never get rich and famous proving that there *isn't* a monster."

"Right," I said. "You could have proved that about Lake Michigan and saved a bundle in travel expenses."

"Well," he said with a shrug, "at least science will soon be able to state conclusively that it's just another legend with no basis in fact."

"Seems a pity, though," I said, "after all that effort."

"I agree," he said. "Finding the monster would have been the biggest news since Stanley found Livingstone."

"Bigger," I said. "Doctor Livingstone was merely misplaced, but everybody knew he existed."

"All right, bigger," agreed Nelson. "But it doesn't exist, and that's that."

"Brother Nelson," I said, "my heart goes out to you, as one Christian to another. I appreciate all the hard work you've gone to trying to scare up the monster, all the expense and privation you put up with, and I have it within my power to do you a favor for which I think you'll be everlastingly grateful."

"Oh?" he said.

"Yeah," I said, pulling the packet of photos out of my pocket and shoving them across the table to him. "I got something here that just might interest you."

"You do?" he said, picking up the packet and opening it.

"Well?" I said, as he thumbed through the photos. "What do you think?"

He stared at me for a long minute and then said, "All right. I'm interested."

"I kind of thought you might be," I said, shooting him a great big Sunday-go-to-meeting grin. "What would it be worth if I was to put you right next to her?"

"I've never indulged in this kind of transaction before," he said. "What do you think it's worth?"

"I know scientists ain't exactly loaded down with cash," I said sympathetically. "I think five hundred dollars would do for now. We can renegotiate after you're rich and famous."

He looked at a couple of the photos again. "Five hundred seems a little steep," he said.

"All right," I said. "Because I got nothing but trust in my fellow man, three hundred."

He considered it for a moment, then dug into his wallet and pulled out six fifty dollar bills.

"Brother Nelson," I said, "you ain't gonna regret this."

"I'd better not," he said. "Shall we go right now?"

"She's just finished eating," I said. "Let's give her a few hours to digest her meal, and then we'll go get her. Why don't I meet you at your boat at, say, two this afternoon?"

"I don't feel like waiting," he said.

"I'm telling you, she's been eating all night," I said. "She's gonna be all sluggish right now."

"I don't care," said Nelson stubbornly. "A deal is a deal."

"I'll tell you what," I said. "I can understand you being so anxious to get a look at her, after being up here alone on the lake all this time. Since you're so all-fired eager, why don't you go looking for her now, and if you ain't found her by two o'clock, come on back to your boat."

"She'd better be there," he said, getting to his feet.

"You got my word on it, Brother Nelson," I told him as he walked out of the dining room.

I spent most of the morning walking around town, looking for the best place to build my tabernacle, and finally hit on a spot right between two taverns, which seemed a likely place to attract sinners as they staggered from one bar to the other, and then I had lunch and went on down to Loch Ness. I found Nelson's boat, and waited next to it until sunset. I couldn't figure out what was keeping him, since I knew he didn't know how to attract Nessie but finally I went back to Glen Mohr and asked if he'd returned there.

"Actually, he checked out at noon, sir," said the clerk.

"Yeah?"

He nodded. "And the young lady was with him."

"What young lady?"

"Anna, the gamekeeper's daughter. I believe they were going off to Glasgow to get married."

"Well, if that don't beat all," I said. "I wonder how in tunket he managed to run into her?"

"I believe *you* can claim the credit for that, sir," said the clerk with a smile.

"Me?"

He pulled out a few of the photos I had taken of Anna. "Mr. Nelson showed these to me on his way out, and asked me to identify the building in the background. Well, as anyone could have told him, it's Culloden House. He left in rather a hurry, and returned a few hours later with Anna on his arm."

Just then a kind of pudgy gentleman in a constable's uniform burst into Glen Mohr and walked up to me.

"Are you Lucifer Jones?" he demanded.

"The Right Reverend Doctor Lucifer Jones, at your service," I said.

"Doctor Jones, you're under arrest!"

"What the hell for?" I demanded.

He handed me a batch of photos of Nessie eating the fish guts. "Did you take these?"

"Ain't nothing illegal about taking pictures, is there?" I said.

"But it *is* illegal to fish in the laird's loch," said the constable. He sighed and shook his head. "What I can't understand is why, if you had to break the law, you added insult to injury by sending the photographic proof of it to his gamekeeper."

Well, we argued back and forth for about five more minutes, but in the end I was carted off to the local hoosegow, where I languished alone until dinnertime, when Angus McNair and his buddies heard about what had happened and snuck me in some poached salmon, which truth to tell wasn't worth all the buildup they had given it.

Then, just before midnight, the constable unlocked my cell and escorted me out to the front door of the jailhouse.

"Doctor Jones, you're free to go," he said.

"You finally figured out that you got no legal right to hold me, huh?" I said, brushing myself off.

"I have every legal right to hold you," he said, "but the laird's gamekeeper, in celebration of his daughter's pending marriage, has declared an amnesty for all the local poachers." He lowered his voice. "I've done a little bit of digging around, and if I were you, I'd get out of town before her father, who's about the best shot in the county, finds out exactly how and why his daughter met her future husband, and what her relationship was to the matchmaker."

It struck me as right good advice, and truth to tell, I'd had my fill of rainy weather and fish guts, and me and the Lord decided it was time to set off once again to find the perfect location for our tabernacle.

10. A TABERNACLE IS NOT A HOME

After my little misadventures with the Clubfoot of Notre Dame and the Crown Jewels of England and the Loch Ness Monster, I was fast running out of European countries in which to establish my tabernacle—and even before that, I was in serious danger of running out of continents on which my presence was allowed. I'd heard tell that Germany had a steady supply of good beer, and since preaching can be mighty thirsty work, I made up my mind that no matter what happened, I was setting up shop there.

The newspapers were full of the antics of some little housepainter who had already corralled most of the sinners in Berlin, so I decided to head over to Hamburg, where I was assured I'd find a passel of souls in serious need of salvation.

As soon as I got there, I started wandering the streets of the city, looking for the proper location for my tabernacle. It didn't take too long to figure out that most of the folks were heading for the Reeperbahn, which was an area loaded down with bars and nightclubs, and I figured that it didn't make much sense bringing Mohammed to the mountain since Mohammed was having a high old time right where he was, so I decided to look around for some For Sale signs, and after a few minutes I turned onto a little street called Herbertstrasse, the likes of which I ain't never encountered before or since.

What it was was a bunch of buildings, each with three or four great big windows down on the ground level, and in each window was a pretty young German lady in her unmentionables, and for some reason not a single one of 'em had remembered to pull the shades down, and whenever I'd look in and offer 'em a smile of detached artistic appreciation, they'd smile right back at me.

Well, I hadn't gotten halfway down the block when I decided that Herbertstrasse seemed just the place to establish my tabernacle, since it was close to the Reeperbahn, which would supply me with a steady stream of sinners, and it was filled with a bunch of friendly neighbors of the female persuasion who kept smiling at anyone who happened to walk by.

As long as my mind was made up, I figured there wasn't no sense in wasting time, so I walked up to a blonde lady who was sitting by an open window, enjoying the cool evening breeze, to ask her if any of the buildings on the street happened to be for sale.

"Good evening, ma'am," I said.

"Hi, handsome," she replied in a thick German accent. "I am Helga."

"Pleased to make your acquaintance, Helga," I said. "I'm the Right Reverend Doctor Lucifer Jones. Do you know if any of these here hostelries is for sale?"

She just stared at me and frowned, like she couldn't understand simple American.

"The buildings, Helga," I said.

"Buildings?" she repeated.

"Yeah," I said. "Are any of 'em for sale, and if so, for how much?"

"Ah!" she said, her face brightening. "How much?"

"Yeah."

"Thirty marks," said Helga.

"Thirty marks?" I said. "You're kidding!"

She shrugged. "Okay, twenty five marks."

"Twenty five marks for *everything*?" I asked.

"For *everything*, thirty marks."

Well, I didn't want no one to move out the furniture or the refrigerator, so I figured I might as well buy the whole place, lock, stock, and barrel, since it was such a cheap price for such a nice building.

"Who do I pay?" I asked.

"You pay *me*," said Helga. "Wait and I open door."

A minute later the front door opened and she grabbed me by the arm and yanked me in off the street.

"You pay me now," she said.

"I kind of thought I'd take a look around first," I said. "You know, kind of inspect the plumbing and the heating and the necessaries and all."

"You pay me now," she repeated.

"Well, what the hell," I said, counting out the money and handing it over, "for thirty marks, how badly can I get took?"

Well, take my word for it, I never in all my experience found a person to be so grateful to make a cut-rate real estate sale. She practically dragged me up the stairs and into her bedroom, and before too long we got to know each other about as well as two people *can* get to know each other on such short notice. Helga kept shrieking and screaming like all get out, and I kept trying to shush her up so we didn't bother the other tenants, but when I finally got her to keep quiet I heard all kind of yells and giggles coming from down the hall, and I figured either all the young ladies were entertaining their gentleman friends at the same time or else they had contracted some rare but contagious disease in which screaming and laughing were the two main symptoms.

When we were all done, Helga climbed back into what she was wearing when I'd made her acquaintance and walked back downstairs, but I figured now that I owned the building I'd take a little tour of it, so I walked down the corridor, hoping I wouldn't catch no giggling disease, and pretty soon I came to a kitchen where about half a dozen blonde German ladies were gathered, most of 'em drinking beer or coffee.

"Good day to you, ladies," I said.

"Who are you?" asked one of 'em in somewhat better English than Helga's.

"I'm the Right Reverend Doctor Lucifer Jones," I said. "Are you just visiting, or do you all live here?"

Well, she laughed aloud at that, which made me figure maybe I was right about the disease, and when she was all through giggling she said, "We work here."

"In the kitchen?" I said. "Just how many cooks does this place hire?"

Well, she cracked up again, and this time she translated it into German, and everyone else started laughing, and I figured that the first thing I'd better do the next morning was stop by a doctor's office and get some kind of vaccination if it wasn't already too late.

"Now let me ask you, Reverend Jones," said the lady who spoke English, "what are *you* doing here?"

"I just bought the place," I said.

"You?" she said, looking kind of surprised.

"Right," I said. "I was kind of hoping for something with maybe a steeple, but there just wasn't no way I could turn it down for the price."

"Do you know what this place is?" she asked.

"As near as I can tell, it's an apartment building what's badly in need of window-shades and soundproofing," I said. "But once I clean it up and give it a paint job, it's gonna be the Tabernacle of Saint Luke."

"A tabernacle?" she repeated. "In *Herbertstrasse*?" Suddenly she started laughing again.

"What's so rib-tickling about that?" I asked.

"Reverend Jones, there is nothing in Herbertstrasse but whorehouses!"

"Yeah?"

"Yes."

"You know," I said, "I *thought* all them young ladies in the windows was dressed a little light for this time of year."

"Now that you've bought the place, what is to become of us?" she asked.

"Well, I wouldn't never want it said that a place of worship threw the flowers of German womanhood out into the street," I answered.

"You mean we can keep on working here?"

"Why not?"

"It seems somehow inconsistent with running a tabernacle," she said.

"Nonsense," I said. "A tabernacle can't function without sinners. If there's a better way to attract 'em, I ain't never come across it."

"Reverend Jones," she said with a great big grin, "I think we're all going to get along just fine."

"Never occurred to me that we wouldn't," I replied, grinning right back at her.

"We've been turning over fifty percent of our earnings to the former owner," she said. "How much will *you* charge?"

"As a gesture of goodwill, the Tabernacle of Saint Luke only wants forty percent," I said.

"It's a deal."

"You know," I said, "now that I come to think of it, I ain't got no place to stay. I'll be happy to lower it to thirty percent for any one of you frail flowers who'll give me a night's shelter."

Well, once she translated it I was overwhelmed with offers of shelter along with friendly, nurturing care, and my faith in the generosity and compassion of my fellow man—or in this case, my fellow woman—was reaffirmed.

I got up bright and early the next morning and went to a local sign painter and had him fix me up a sign that told one and all that they were about to enter the Tabernacle of Saint Luke, and I had him do it in German, French, Italian and English, just so we didn't lose no sinners that couldn't read a foreign tongue. Then I had him add that the casual sinner who entered the Tabernacle could find salvation, free beer, and a batch of friendly, caring young ladies who would be happy to listen to his confessions and even help him come up with some new ones.

Once the sign was up and we were open for business, I took over the ground floor living room, set up a pulpit, and let it be known that I planned to spread the word of the Lord from 8:00 to 8:05 every evening, and maybe even oftener if the situation called for it. Hamburg was another town that hadn't never heard of bingo, but I found an old roulette wheel in a secondhand shop and announced that every Tuesday and Thursday we'd be indulging in friendly little games of chance to raise funds for our overseas missions.

Things went along pretty well for the first week, and even better the second, and I got to thinking that if business kept up like this, I was going to have to start four or five more tabernacles on Herbertstrasse.

I took to spending my mornings in the city's parks, recruiting handmaidens for the congregation, and I did my serious sleeping in the afternoons, when the salvation business was at its slowest. Then word got out that the Tabernacle of Saint Luke was charging ten percent less overhead for such business arrangements as the local females were inclined to make, and suddenly we had a steady stream of blonde ladies applying for positions with the tabernacle. Interviewing 'em was exhausting work, if you catch my meaning, but I figured it was my own special burden, so I done it with nary a complaint, and pretty soon we had three full eight-hour shifts of handmaidens toiling away in the service of the Lord, and an awful lot of the windows in the other buildings were temporarily boarded up.

Then one night I came down the stairs after a vigorous afternoon's nap, and who should I find waiting for me there but Rupert Cornwall.

"Well, howdy, Brother Rupert," I said. "I ain't seen you since we was both courting Lady Edith Quilton back in India."

"Doctor Jones!" he said. "What in the world are *you* doing here?"

"Just spreading the word of the Lord," I answered. "How about yourself?"

"Well, it's a strange situation," he said. "I *own* this building. I've been away for a month, tending to other matters, and I just arrived back not ten minutes ago to find some interloper claims to have bought it."

"I hate to correct you, Brother Rupert," I said, "but I ain't no interloper, and it just so happens that I'm the landlord of these here premises."

"*You?*"

"That's right," I said.

"Who do you think you bought it from?" he demanded.

"Helga."

"Helga's a goddamned prostitute!" yelled Rupert.

"I'll thank you not to use the Lord's name in vain when you're in the Tabernacle of Saint Luke," I said.

"What the hell makes you think Helga had any right to sell this building?" he continued.

"I negotiated it fair and square," I said.

"How much did you pay for it?" he asked.

"Thirty marks."

"*Thirty marks?*" he screamed. "It's worth seventy-five thousand!"

"I thought it was a mite inexpensive myself," I said, "but that don't change the fact that it's mine."

"Where is your bill of sale?" said Rupert.

"It was an informal transaction," I said.

"It was an illegal transaction!" he yelled. "This place belongs to me!"

"Why don't we let the tenants take a vote on who they want to be their landlord?" I suggested.

"They have nothing to do with this! This is my building, and I want you out of here in the next thirty minutes."

"Look, Brother Rupert, I don't see no reason why a couple of old friends like you and me can't work this out."

"We can work it out just fine," he said. "Get off my premises."

"Well, I suppose I could clear out," I said.

"Good."

"Of course," I added, "I ain't got no place to go, and I imagine the local constabularies would pick me up for vagrancy before long, and being the good-natured and friendly man of the cloth that I am, I'd probably try to entertain 'em with some amusing stories while they were fingerprinting me down at the station, and one of the ones that comes to mind is how you stole the Empire Emerald back in Hong Kong, and after we'd shared a laugh or two over that, I might tell 'em how you tried to get your hands on the Flame of Bharatpur when we was in Rajasthan, and sooner or later we'd share a drink or two and I'd tell 'em why you can't never go back to Australia, and that there's still half a dozen warrants out for your arrest."

"That's outrageous!" he said. "Does our friendship mean nothing to you?"

"I cherish our friendship, Brother Rupert," I told him. "But on the other hand, *I* ain't the one who's trying to throw *you* out into the street."

"Doctor Jones," he said. "*Lucifer*, my old friend. Suddenly I feel certain that we can work something out."

"Well, that's right friendly of you, Brother Rupert," I said. "And I want you to know that despite our little contretemps, I never doubted that you was a decent Christian who would do the right thing sooner or later."

"All right," he said with a sigh. "Promise not to go to the police, and you can have a quarter of the take."

"I'm ashamed of you, Brother Rupert," I said. "When you flim-flam *me*, you're flim-flamming the Lord. And betwixt us, me and the Lord have tripled the business in less than a month."

"All right," he said. "A third."

"Sixty percent," I said.

"I can't let you buy more than half my business for thirty marks!"

"You're looking at it all wrong," I said. "I'm *giving* you almost half *my* business for nothing."

Well, we argued and haggled for another hour, and in the end it was decided that I owned fifty percent of the voting stock in the Tabernacle of Saint Luke, Rupert owned the other fifty percent, and the Lord held an option on three hundred shares of preferred non-voting stock.

Things went along pretty well for the next week. Rupert had taken a room for himself at the Vier Jahreszeiten Hotel, which was a fancy place in the center of town, but I couldn't see no reason to move out of the tabernacle, where I could keep in close contact with all them flowers of German womanhood who were toiling day and night in the service of the Lord, and whenever it looked like one of 'em might fall from grace I saw to it that I was always first in line with an uplifting word and a little missionary work.

We were making so much money that I decided some new preaching clothes were in order, so I stopped by a local tailor and had him make me up a white silk suit, which I figured would reflect the purity of my thoughts, and I also got a couple of nifty green and red and gold Hawaiian shirts to go with it, just to make some of the sailors from the South Seas who stopped by feel more at home.

Then I figured that as since I was now sharing the take with Rupert Cornwall, it wouldn't hurt none to do a little advertising to bring in even more sinners, so I made up a bunch of signs directing people to the Tabernacle of Saint Luke and posted 'em all over the Reeperbahn, so folks would know where to go to get their sins redeemed.

All this time I was sweating and toiling in the service of the Lord, I hadn't seen hide nor hair of Rupert Cornwall, except for his nightly visit to collect his share of the money, and truth to tell I was feeling a little resentful that me and God were doing all this work for only half the profits, but being the big-hearted Christian gentleman that I am I kept my feelings to myself, except when the handmaidens would ask why he was still hanging around after I had bought the place, and I had to explain to 'em that the Lord teaches us to be charitable to sinners, though it wasn't a piece of advice I necessarily wanted them to live by, so I further explained that that particular passage was only in the Australian translation of the Good Book and since Rupert was the only Australian they knew, it didn't really apply to none of the other sinners who visited the tabernacle with money to spend.

Then one night, while Rupert was upstairs counting out his share of the money, a group of ten real well-dressed guys walked in all at once, and each and every one of 'em looked kind of unhappy, like life hadn't been treating 'em none too well of late.

"Welcome to the Tabernacle of Saint Luke, gents," I said, walking over to 'em. "Most of our handmaidens is otherwise occupied at the moment, but if you'd like, I can whip through a quick service and get you a head start on your salvation so's you'll have a few sins paid for in advance."

"Never mind that," said the littlest one of the group. "Do you know who we are?"

"It don't make no difference to the Tabernacle of Saint Luke," I said. "We treat all sinners the same, regardless of race, creed, or political affiliation."

"We are the other landlords of Herbertstrasse," continued the little guy, "and it is not inaccurate to say that we are seriously displeased with this establishment."

"You stole our girls!" shouted another.

"And our customers!" yelled a third.

"In other words," said the little guy, "we don't mind a little friendly competition, but you, sir, are a monopolist."

"That's a lie!" I said. "I ain't never shot a king or a prince in my life!"

He just stared at me for a minute and shook his head.

"We have come to buy you out," he said at last.

"The Tabernacle of Saint Luke ain't for sale," I said.

"You're quite certain of that?" he asked me.

"Lemme put it this way," I said; "If I was you, I wouldn't go laying no serious bets against it."

"You have complicated our task," he said sadly. "We came here to make you a legitimate business offer, and you refuse even to listen to it. That leaves us no other choice but to take over your business by other means."

And suddenly I was staring into the business ends of ten pistols.

"It just so happens that the judge of the local probate court is my brother-in-law," said the little guy. "If something were to happen to you, something shall we say permanent, I think it not unlikely that he would decide to award your possessions to myself and my associates."

Just then Rupert appeared at the head of the stairs, having counted out and pocketed his share of the previous day's income, and suddenly I saw a way out of my predicament.

"I'm sorry, gentlemen," said Rupert, climbing down to the main floor, "but we don't allow firearms in here."

"Who's he?" asked the little guy.

"Gents," I said, "this is Mr. Rupert Cornwall, formerly of Australia, Hong Kong, and India. Brother Rupert, these here fellers are associated with the local court system, and are looking into the ownership of the Tabernacle of Saint Luke."

"Oh?" he said, with a kind of greedy smile on his face.

"Yeah," I said. "Just tell 'em I bought it fair and square and you can be on your way."

"I hate to correct you, Doctor Jones," said Rupert, "but I am, and always have been, the owner of this building."

"You don't have to pretend for my sake, Brother Rupert," I said. "Just tell 'em the truth."

"The truth is that you are a mountebank who has no legal claim to these premises," said Rupert.

I turned to the little guy. "Well, I done my best," I said.

"You are free to leave," he said, and then turned to Rupert. "Mr. Cornwall, I wonder if my associates and I might have a word in private with you. We have a business proposition to make."

"Oh?" said Rupert.

"Well, two propositions, actually," he said with a smile.

Rupert led 'em into the next room, and I figured that whichever proposition he took, my stake in the Tabernacle of Saint Luke was up in flames, so I went up to my room, collected my money, kissed Helga and the other handmaidens good bye, and headed off for fresh territory, confident that having got my feet wet in the Tabernacle business, so to speak, I'd do even better with the next one.

11. DEATH IN THE AFTERNOON

There are a lot of ways to see Spain. In my expert opinion, the very worst of them is to be standing in the middle of the arena at the Plaza de Toros while a bull named El Diablo is pawing the dirt about twenty feet away and planning to use you for target practice.

But I'm getting a little bit ahead of myself.

If you ever go to Madrid, you're going to make two discoveries right quick: all the women wear black, and all the men think they're bullfighters. Beyond that it's pretty much like any other city, except that the people there don't speak much American, and they all go crazy for this kind of Spanish tap dance which is always being done by guys in tight pants called Juan or Jose or Diego.

I'd left Berlin with a healthy supply of money in my wallet, so I decided to check in at the finest hotel in town, which back in them days was the Palace. There were posters all over the lobby about something called the Fiesta de Toros, which as near as I could translate meant that the restaurant had bought too much steak and was trying to find ways to get rid of it, but I wasn't hungry anyway, so instead I moseyed out onto the street and wandered around until sunset, and then, because wandering can be pretty thirsty work, I stopped by a little tavern about a mile from the hotel.

The place was just about empty, except for this tall, athletic-looking feller with slicked-down hair and a big black mustache who was sitting at the bar, and when he saw me he sort of waved me over to join him.

"May I buy you a drink?" he asked.

"Why, that's right neighborly of you, Brother," I said, sitting down next to him.

"You are English?" he asked.

"American," I said. "The Right Reverend Honorable Doctor Lucifer Jones, at your service."

"You have come a day too soon," he said morosely. "The service will be held tomorrow night."

"Yeah?" I said, wondering what service he was talking about.

He nodded. "The women will be wailing in the streets, and they will throw themselves upon the coffin. Ten thousand candles will be lit at the cathedral, strong men will weep, and little children will lose their faith in God. The line to the cemetery will be two miles long, and the Cardinal himself will speak at the graveside."

"Sounds impressive," I allowed.

"It will be a funeral they will talk about for years," he agreed.

"Uh...pardon my ignorance, but I'm a stranger in town," I said. "Who's about to die—some president or general or such?"

"Me," he said glumly.

"You?"

"I am Pablo Francisco de Varga," he said. "Perhaps you have heard of me?"

"Didn't you used to play third base for the Brooklyn Dodgers?" I said.

"I am the greatest bullfighter of all time," he said.

"Excuse a personal question, Brother Pablo," I said, "but why are you figuring on dying tomorrow?"

"El Diablo," he said.

"What is that—some kind of disease?" I asked, backing away a bit just in case it was catching.

"El Diablo is the bull I must face tomorrow in the Fiesta de Toros," he said. "He has already killed three matadors."

"Well, I'm right sorry to hear that," I said. "But if you're the greatest bullfighter around, what makes you think you're gonna lose?"

"I have broken a bone in my foot," he said. "I am completely unable to move to the side. El Diablo will kill me on my very first *veronica*."

"Why don't you call it off, then?" I said.

"Tens of thousands of people have come to see Varga face El Diablo in the arena," he said with dignity. "I will not disappoint them."

"Seems to me you're just about guaranteed to disappoint them what ain't rooting for the bull," I said. "If I was you, I'd get a doctor's excuse or whatever it takes to postpone this thing."

"That is because you are not a Spaniard," said Varga. "You do not understand the concept of honor. This is a matter between El Diablo and myself. I will not be the first to back down."

Well, we got to talking and drinking, and he kept explaining the Spanish concept of honor, which seemed an awful lot like the American concept of stupidity, but after a couple of hours I gave up trying to talk him out of it, and after he'd finished a whole bottle of whiskey and paid for mine as well, I figured the least I could do to thank him was help him hobble back to his hotel. He was right insistent that no one see him limping, so we snuck around to the back door and went in through the kitchen and found a freight elevator, and a few minutes later I left him and returned to the Palace.

It seemed to me that as long as I couldn't talk him out of canceling the fight, there wasn't no reason why I shouldn't make a little profit out of it, since me and God still planned to build our tabernacle and I didn't know what construction costs were like in Madrid, so I walked up to the desk clerk and asked him where the local bookmaker had set up shop. He must have misunderstood, because what he sent me to was a publishing company, but as I was walking back to the hotel I passed by a casino, and I figured if anyone knew where I could lay some bets on the bullfight, this was the place.

I walked in, and sure enough, along with poker and craps and roulette tables, they had a guy in the corner taking bets on the big bullfight, but the only odds he was giving was on whether Varga would be awarded one ear, both ears, or both ears and the tail.

"Good evening," I said, walking up to him.

"*Buenas noches,*" he replied.

"Well, that's right kind of you, but I've already et," I said. "I'm just here to make a sporting wager on the big bullfight tomorrow."

"Yes, *senor?*" he said. "And what do you choose?"

"I don't see no odds on El Diablo winning," I said.

He laughed so hard I thought he was gonna fall right off his chair, and when he finally got ahold of himself, he wiped the tears from his face and smiled at me.

"You have a wonderful sense of humor, *senor,*" he said.

"Yeah, I been told that many a time," I said modestly. "But I still want to lay a bet on El Diablo."

"Do you know that El Diablo is facing the great Pablo Francisco de Varga?"

"Who's he?" I said.

Suddenly he got a greedy gleam in his eye. "All right, *senor*," he said. "I will give you odds of ten to one."

I pulled out my wad and counted out all but about two hundred dollars of it.

"Okay," I said. "I'll put twelve thousand on El Diablo to win."

Suddenly there was a hushed silence in the room. The guy I'd been talking to looked at me like I was crazy, but finally he shrugged, took my money, and wrote me out a receipt.

"You are a fool," he said. "Varga is the greatest matador of all time, greater even than Juan Belmonte."

"Well, for all you know, El Diablo is greater than Babe the Blue Ox," I said.

"Than *who*?"

Well, I could tell I was talking to a cultural illiterate, so I just bade him good bye and went back to the Palace, where I had a couple of drinks to wash down the whiskey I'd had with Varga, and then went up to my room and took a shower. I had just climbed out of the tub and dried off when I heard the door open, so I looked out from the bathroom and found three well-dressed Spaniards sitting around the room, one of 'em normal sized and two of 'em looking like gorillas with suits on.

"Howdy, Brothers," I said. "What can I do for you?"

"You are the Reverend Lucifer Jones?" asked the normal one.

"The Right Reverend Doctor Lucifer Jones," I corrected him.

"Then we have come to the right place," he said. "We have some business to discuss."

"Well, given the time of day, I'm afraid I'm gonna have to charge you time and a half for salvation," I said. "Though if any of you are lately bereaved, I got a group rate for funerals."

"Allow me to introduce myself," he said. "I am Manuel Garcia, and these are my two associates. You may call them Mr. Crush and Mr. Smash." Mr. Crush smiled at me, and from where I sat it looked like he had steel teeth; Mr. Smash just glared sullenly. "Did you just bet twelve thousand dollars that Pablo Francisco de Varga would be killed in the arena tomorrow?" continued Garcia.

"You make it sound kind of morbid," I said. "I didn't so much bet *against* him as I bet *for* El Diablo."

"My colleagues and I would like to know *why* you bet against the great Varga."

"Because I think the bull will win," I said.

"Do not play games with us, Reverend Jones," said Garcia. "We represent some of the most powerful men in Madrid."

"You're the lawyers for a bunch of weightlifters?" I asked.

"Enough of this foolishness!" snapped Garcia. "You have bet a substantial sum on El Diablo. We, too, are gamblers, and we want to know if you are privy to some inside information that would lead you to make a wager that, on the face of it, seems laughably foolish."

"Well, I don't see no point in lying to you," I said. "But to be totally honest and even-handed about it, I don't see no point in confiding to you, neither. I mean, it ain't as if you was regular parishioners who had promised to donate, say, five thousand dollars apiece to the Tabernacle of Saint Luke once this here contest betwixt man and beast reaches its possibly tragic conclusion."

"All right, Reverend Jones," said Garcia. "We agree to your terms. Give us your information, and if we elect to make our wagers based upon it and Varga should lose, we will deliver fifteen thousand dollars to you at the conclusion of the event."

"Well, that's mighty agreeable of you," I said, "but how do I know I can trust you to keep your word?"

The three of 'em looked like I'd just stabbed their mothers.

"We are Spaniards," said Garcia. "We live and die by our code of honor."

"All right," I said. "But I want to sit with you guys at the bullfight, just so it don't slip your minds."

"Men have died for lesser insults, Reverend Jones," growled Mr. Crush in broken English.

"Painfully," added Mr. Smash.

"And men have gone hungry for lesser precautions," I said. "Have we got a deal?"

They whispered amongst themselves in Spanish, and finally all three looked at me and nodded.

"Okay," I said. "I happened to run into Pablo Francisco de Varga in a bar earlier tonight, and he's already making plans for his funeral."

"But why?" demanded Garcia. "Surely the great Varga has not lost his courage!"

"Unthinkable!" added the other two.

"What he's done is gone and busted a bone in his foot, and for some crazy reason he don't want to tell no one or call the match off," I said.

"Well, of course not," agreed Garcia. "He has lived by the code; he will die by it."

"You don't find that a mite peculiar?" I asked.

"Absolutely not. We shall pass along your information to our principals, and I'm sure they will act accordingly." He stood up. "Thank you for your time, Reverend Jones."

"Where will I meet you guys tomorrow?" I said.

"We will be waiting outside the box office at the Plaza de Toros," said Garcia, and then the three of 'em walked out, and I finished drying myself off and spent a little time figuring out just how much money I'd be worth after poor Varga went off to the great bullfight plaza in the sky, and finally I climbed under the covers and went to sleep and dreamed about building my tabernacle right next to Varga's grave as a way of thanking him for putting me onto this opportunity.

I woke up bright and early at about noontime, got dressed, and caught a cab out to the Plaza de Toros, where true to his word, Manuel Garcia was waiting for me with Mr. Crush and Mr. Smash. The four of us went to his private box, where we had a few beers and watched a couple of warm-up fights, and by the time the Big Event rolled around the score was Matadors 2, Bulls 0.

We sat there and chatted about this and that, and after awhile we became aware of a kind of uneasy murmuring in the crowd, and when half an hour had passed Garcia said something to Mr. Crush, who left the box and returned about five minutes later to whisper something in Garcia's ear.

"Come with me," said Garcia, getting to his feet.

"I think I'd rather stay here, sipping my beer and getting a little sun," I said.

"Come with me!" he repeated, and suddenly Mr. Crush grabbed me by one arm and Mr. Smash grabbed me by the other, and I didn't have no choice but to accompany them, since they were holding me a few inches off the ground and rushing to keep up with Garcia.

We came to a door beneath the grandstand, and Garcia nodded to the guard, who let the four of us in. Then we went down a long corridor past a number of dressing rooms, and stopped at one with

Varga's name on the door. Garcia pushed it open, and there on the floor lay Pablo Francisco de Varga, still in his street clothes.

"Is he dead?" I asked.

"Drunk," said Mr. Crush.

Garcia knelt down next to him and slapped his face a few times. He didn't move a muscle.

"We have a serious problem," said Garcia, standing up and facing me.

"Seems to me that Varga's the one with the problem," I said.

"We have bet more than half a million dollars on El Diablo," he said. "If Varga does not appear in the arena, they will cancel the fight."

"Well, it ain't a consummation devoutly to be wished," I allowed. "But on the other hand, it beats losing our money."

"You do not understand," said Garcia. "I have promised some very powerful men that they would increase their money tenfold by wagering on El Diablo. These are not men who like to be disappointed."

"Well, El Diablo is gonna win by a forfeit," I said.

"The bookmakers do not pay off on forfeits," answered Garcia. "No, *someone* must go into the ring and lose to El Diablo. The question is: *who?*"

Suddenly I became aware of the fact that he and Mr. Crush and Mr. Smash were all staring intently at me.

"Oh, no," I said. "You ain't gonna get *me* in a ring with El Diablo! I ain't never fought a bull before!"

"Then you are precisely the person we need," said Garcia. "I have guaranteed my principals that El Diablo cannot lose."

"Then you tell your principals that they're gonna have to learn to live with disappointment," I said. "Nothing's gonna get me to step into that ring!"

"My dear Reverend Jones," he said, and suddenly Mr. Crush and Mr. Smash were pointing their revolvers right betwixt my eyeballs, "you have two admittedly unhappy choices: you can die in the arena amid the cheers of thousands, or you can die in the next ten seconds, alone and un-mourned. I am afraid that there is simply no third alternative."

Which is how I came to be standing in the middle of the Plaza de Toros in Madrid in a fancy bullfighting outfit while El Diablo stared at me through his beady little eyes and pawed the dirt.

Since I was supposed to lose, Garcia hadn't seen fit to give me a sword, so all I had with me was a red cape called a *muleta*. I was more than a little bit nervous at the prospect of hobnobbing with the Lord in person in the next few minutes, and my hands were shaking, and this made the *muleta* shake, and for some reason this annoyed the bejabbers out of El Diablo, who snorted and drooled a bit and then let out a bellow and ran straight toward me.

Well, I figured if he wanted the *muleta* all that badly, *I* sure wasn't going to argue none about it, so I just dropped it on the ground and ran to the far side of the arena while he shredded the thing with his horns and everyone started whistling, though truth to tell I couldn't spot no melody.

After he'd worked off a little excess energy on the *muleta*, El Diablo lifted his head and looked around, and when his eyes fell on me he pawed the dirt a couple of more times and then lowered his head and charged, and I made a dash for the grandstand and reached it about two steps ahead of him and flung myself into the first row while El Diablo plowed into the concrete wall that protected the customers and busted off one of his horns.

He looked a little bleary eyed as he backed off, and I figured I might as well stay where I was for the rest of the afternoon, but then Mr. Crush and Mr. Smash made their way through the crowd and reached my side and tossed me back into the ring, and El Diablo shot them an appreciative look and started sizing me up again.

I climbed back onto my feet just as he charged, and as he lowered his head I grabbed ahold of his remaining horn on the assumption that he couldn't stab me with it as long as I kept it at arm's length, but then he tossed his head and lifted me way off the ground, and suddenly I found myself sitting on his back. He came to a stop and stared all around the arena, looking for me, while I stayed where I was and tried to figure out what to do next.

Well, neither of us moved for the next couple of minutes, and all of a sudden the crowd started throwing popcorn boxes and beer bottles into the ring and whistling some more, and finally El Diablo charged at a piece of paper that was fluttering on the ground and I fell off with a thud, and he wheeled around and started snorting and drooling and bellowing at me again. Since I didn't have no *muleta* left, I quick slipped off the little jacket they had made me wear and held it out to see if maybe he wanted to eat *it* instead of *me*, and he bellowed again and charged straight at it. I let go of it just before he reached it and started running again, only this time I didn't hear no galloping footsteps behind me, so I turned to see what was going on, and what had happened was that he'd stuck his horn into the sleeve of the jacket and pierced right through it, and the rest of it was covering his face so that he couldn't see nothing.

I figured this was as good a time to take my leave as any, and probably better than most, so I walked back to the door through which Mr. Crush and Mr. Smash had dragged me in, but when I got there I found a bunch of guys in bullfighting outfits all laughing their heads off.

"I never knew you could be so funny, Pablo Francisco!" guffawed one of 'em.

"It has been wildly amusing," agreed another, "but now I see that you have come back for your sword. Here it is." He handed me this long sword and kind of pointed me back into the arena and gave me a friendly shove.

El Diablo still hadn't gotten the jacket off his face, and I figured if I was ever gonna kill him and get out of this in one piece, now was probably the ideal time, so I walked cautiously up to him and got all ready to run him through when it occurred to me that I didn't know where his heart was. I had a feeling it was probably somewhere inside his chest, but there was an awful lot of chest in front of me, and I was pretty sure I was only gonna get one chance to do it right before El Diablo finally got rid of the jacket.

I finally made up my mind where to stab him, but then Mr. Crush jumped into the arena and pointed his pistol at me, still determined to win Garcia's bets for him, and just as he fired I ducked and then El Diablo jumped like he'd been shot, which he had, and fell over dead.

Well, the police surrounded Mr. Crush right quick, and he started jabbering something in Spanish and pointing at me, and by the time I'd finished taking a couple of bows and walked back to the dressing room there were a passel of police waiting there for me, and they took me down to the local calaboose and I spent the night there, still in my bullfighting outfit.

They left me in the cell for three days and three nights with no comfort except my well-worn copy of the Good Book, and let me tell you that it was a pretty morose time, since I soon realized that thanks to surviving my ordeal with El Diablo I was destitute again, which was getting to be a common condition but still not one that brought me any great comfort.

Then, on the morning of the fourth day, I was pulled off my cot and out of my cell, and then handcuffed and brung into court and made to stand before the bench, which was being presided over by a judge named Alberto Coronado, who had kind of a lean and hungry look to him, like maybe his shorts were too tight or someone had just got him out of bed.

"So *you* are Lucifer Jones," he said.

"The Right Reverend Honorable Doctor Lucifer Jones," I corrected him. "Pleased to make your acquaintance."

"Are you really?" said Judge Coronado. "I'm fascinated to make yours."

"Well, I'm right flattered to hear it," I said. "Maybe if you could see fit to remove these here handcuffs, we could slip off to a local bar and lift a few and swap stories."

"I think not," he said. "It seems we have a little business to get through first."

"We do?"

He nodded. "You have been charged with conspiring to fix the outcome of a bullfight, and to make an enormous profit thereby. How do you plead?"

"I didn't make no profit at all," I pointed out. "El Diablo lost, may the Lord have mercy on his poor bovine soul."

"That in no way alters the fact that you did everything within your power to predetermine the result. I am afraid I am going to have to find you guilty. Your three friends admitted everything, and are currently serving their own sentences."

"Well, it seems mighty single-minded and unfair to me, Your Honor," I said, "considering that I wound up dead broke and almost got killed in the process."

"I have taken that into account," said Judge Coronado. "I have even made inquiries to see if one of our European neighbors would let us send you there on the condition that you promise never to return to Spain."

"Sounds good to me," I said.

"It sounded good to me, too," admitted Judge Coronado. "Then we started receiving replies from the various governments we contacted." He looked at me and smiled. "You lead quite an interesting life for a man of the cloth."

"Well, you know how it is," I said modestly.

"I truly had no idea how it was," he replied. "Though I do now." He began riffling through some papers. "It seems that you are wanted in Roumania for grave robbing, and in Germany for running a bawdy house."

"Yeah, well, I can explain that," I said.

"The Italians want you for pretending to be an exorcist, and the Hungarian SPCA wants to question you about your treatment of a certain show-dog."

"A series of misunderstandings," I said.

"The French are after you for running an illegal gambling operation in the Cathedral of Notre Dame." He paused and looked at me. "*Notre Dame?*"

"I thought it was a football stadium."

"The government of Crete wishes to speak to you about your complicity in the death of a Professor Zachariah MacDonald, the Scotch claim you are an undesirable who left the country over a game poaching scandal, the British have decided you had something to do with the break-in at a jewelry store on Bond Street, and the new democratically elected government of Sylvania is after you for impersonating a member of the former Royal Family."

"They *asked* me to!" I said heatedly.

Judge Coronado held up a hand for silence. "Finally, the government of Greece has issued a warrant for your arrest for illegally removing salvaged treasure from their country."

"I didn't remove nothing!" I said. "Wait til you hear *my* side of it!"

"Doctor Jones, I'm sure hearing your side of the story would prove most entertaining," said Judge Coronado, "but it doesn't negate the fact that you are a walking disaster. As a responsible member of the European community, I could not in good conscience turn you loose upon our neighbors."

"Then send me somewhere else," I said.

"That is my intention," he said. "Unfortunately, it appears that you have been barred from the continents of North America, Africa and Asia." He paused and stared at me. "You have lived less than half your allotted span of years, Doctor Jones, and you are already in danger of running out of land masses that will accept your presence. Fortunately, no one in South America seems to have heard of you, and since that is sufficiently far from Spain, I have elected to send you there. I must confess that I feel enormous sympathy for the remnants of the once-proud Aztec and Mayan civilizations, but this is a matter of survival, and I would be betraying my high office were I to turn you loose in any Western country. Case closed."

"When do I leave?" I asked.

"You will be transferred to Barcelona tomorrow morning," he said. "Your ship leaves two days later." Suddenly he smiled. "And now that the case is officially closed, let me say that I would be delighted to stop by your cell this afternoon and listen to you explain how thirty-three governments on four continents have so erroneously interpreted your good intentions."

Well, true to his word Judge Coronado stopped by, and we lifted a few while I told him of all my adventures and exploits and encounters, and the next day they shipped me to Barcelona, which I hear tell is a lovely town but ain't much to write home about when viewed from the inside of a prison cell, and then they put me on a boat bound for Brazil.

I had done my best to bring the Word of the Lord to the depraved citizens of Europe, and this was the thanks I got for it. Still, I ain't one to discourage easily, so I started making plans to build my tabernacle in South America, which I finally did do four years later. But before me and God set up shop, I stumbled upon more than my share of lost civilizations and high priestesses and strange voodoo rites and revolutions and the like, and I plan to tell you about 'em someday, but writing your memoirs can be pretty tiring work, so I'm heading off now to find some friendly and sympathetic soul of the female persuasion and renew my artistic energies.

∞ The End (Volume Three) ∞

www.ingramcontent.com/pod-product-compliance
Lightning Source LLC
LaVergne TN
LVHW041626070426
835507LV00008B/473